OUTLINE PLAN
OF
HIGHLAND
COUNTY
OHIO
Scale: 2 Miles to an Inch.

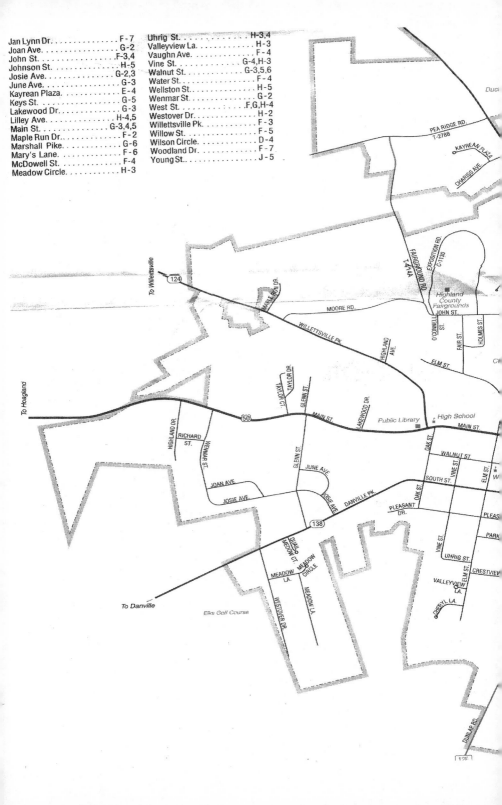

The Hillsboro Story is a multi-voiced tale that brings to light the courageous people who fought for integration and equal protection in the early days of the Civil Rights Movement, at a time when Cold War tensions were at a peak. Anchored by the wisdom of real people who lived through the experience, *The Hillsboro Story* reveals what hides in the shadows of the culture, then and now, and the deep nature of memory as a tool for empowerment and healing.

Like a great epic filmmaker, Susan Banyas moves fluidly between the personal and the historical, the particular and the archetypal, the internal and external. Memory has profound resonance in our time of relative truth, greed and indifference to history. This powerful book is more relevant than ever.

MEREDITH MONK, COMPOSER/ DIRECTOR/ PERFORMER

Susan Banyas left Hillsboro, but Hillsboro never left her—and with this beautifully written book she has recovered a fascinating but forgotten chapter in the history of the civil rights movement.

JON WIENER, PROFESSOR EMERITUS OF HISTORY,
UNIVERSITY OF CA, IRVINE, AUTHOR, *HOW WE FORGOT THE COLD WAR,* CONTRIBUTING EDITOR AT *THE NATION*

Our stories have the power to heal and transform us, but first we must find them and then dance, perform, and dream them with each other and our communities. In the spirit of the best of Studs Terkel, *The Hillsboro Story* is an inspiring model for finding and revealing the lost voices of ordinary and extraordinary people who made our American history.

PAT FERRERO, FILMMAKER, PROFESSOR INTERARTS &
CINEMA, SAN FRANCISCO STATE UNIVERSITY

Weaving her way back and forth, from the early days of the Republic until the present, Banyas has created a history that comes alive with real people whose lives were central to the racial change and backlash, the passions and struggles that engulf this country today.

LEWIS STEEL, CIVIL RIGHT ATTORNEY,
AUTHOR OF *THE BUTLER'S CHILD, A MEMOIR*

THE HILLSBORO STORY

*a kaleidoscope history
of an integration battle
in my hometown*

Susan Grace Banyas

*To Roy
In Light, Susan.
ignite*

SPUYTEN DUYVIL
NEW YORK CITY

ISBN 978-1-947980-90-7 pbk (BW) | 978-1-949966-23-7 (C)

Library of Congress Cataloging-in-Publication Data

Names: Banyas, Susan, author.
Title: The Hillsboro story / Susan Grace Banyas.
Description: New York City : Spuyten Duyvil, [2019] | Includes
    bibliographical references.
Identifiers: LCCN 2018040334 | ISBN 9781947980907
Subjects: LCSH: School integration--Ohio--Hillsboro--Drama. | Hillsboro
    (Ohio)--History--20th century--Drama.
Classification: LCC PS3602.A693 H55 2019 | DDC 812/.6--dc23
LC record available at https://lccn.loc.gov/2018040334

Main Street, Hillsboro, Ohio

Two months after *Brown v. Board of Education* legally ended school segregation, on the night of July 5, 1954, around two a.m., my sleepy segregated little hometown, Hillsboro, Ohio, the county seat of Highland County, was jolted awake by a fire at the colored school; and History and Memory came marching into town like the Fourth of July Parade the day before.

in memory of my mother,
Edith Irene Rhoten Banyas,
a storyteller

Highland County

Histories are never told in isolation.
—Angela Davis

Alley, Hillsboro

Ohio River, from Eden Park, Cincinnati

Walnut Street

OHI-YO

I am eight years old, and women and children appear and disappear outside my third-grade classroom window. They carry signs with messages. OUR CHILDREN PLAY TOGETH-ER, WHY CAN'T THEY LEARN TOGETHER? Why can't they come in? It's snowing outside. I go to the sandbox by the window. I see their coats and shoes, their faces looking back at me. They come every day. All year. No one talks about the trouble on the edge of life, not at school, not at the dinner table. Words float around—*crazy... troublemakers*—then drift on.

There I am, floating in my inner tube in the plastic pool in the backyard on Danville Pike, soaking up the cultural commotion, riding my bike around in it, watching it from behind a window at school, fascinated by the drama, the characters who come and go. But I have no story to hold it, and I remain mute, in the dark, wondering, haunted.

Then the trouble quiets down, but the feeling hums away, the memory settles in.

Outside the snow falls. A chicken is roasting in the oven, stuffed with rosemary. Rosemary is the herb of memory. The memory is set against the backdrop of the Cold War,

Hillsboro, the county seat of Highland County, is nestled in the foothills of the Appalachian Mountains, thirty-eight miles north of the Ohio River, a section of the Mason Dix-on Line that separated the slave state of Kentucky from the "free" state of Ohio, a boundary that John Quincy Adams called, "the title page of a great tragic volume."

The borderlands have an aura, like fog on the road at

night, headlights hugging the dips and curves, eyes fuzzy, nerves rattling. The Memory Place is thick from the Indian Wars, the Civil War, the raids, the secret rooms, the mansions, the shacks, the crazy fears over the years.

I leave Hillsboro, but Hillsboro never leaves me. Spirits tag along, like we're on our way to school, kicking fall leaves, colors flying around and rearranging themselves.

In 2003, I return to my hometown to begin investigating the memory of my first protest. Who are we now? What happened? I need to find the story.

Ancient cartographers found that to represent the world in perspective, they had to draw it in the shape of a heart. One person sends me to the next, and I begin mapping the story by sitting in the living rooms, kitchens, offices, front porches and back yards of the people who share the landscape with me, who color it with their own remembering and generously open up to describe their experiences as mothers, children, spouses, classmates, attorneys, judges, artists, ordinary people, hilarious, eccentric, who acted without apology to set things right for children, for the world.

I write multi-voiced theatre, collaborate with a jazz composer, make a dance history, return the story to the town and the nation. But when the curtain comes down, the story isn't over. Behind the curtain is the backstory, the shadow play, the town's soul story, my soul story, voices in a landscape of origins, the original Ancestors, my Ancestors. "Over here," they whisper, and I follow.

This kaleidoscopic history of a two-year protest in my hometown in the early years of the Civil Rights Movement does not begin or end in the 1950s in Hillsboro, Ohio.

To the Indigenous peoples of the territory, *Ohi-yo* means *great river*, an expression of Nature, a nurturing river flowing through time, the holy presence of creation, a boundless form. The boundary between us—a river, a window—is an illusion *and* a force of nature. The stories we share are ever-changing, born again into the new light.

Webster School

The struggle of man against power
is the struggle of memory against forgetting.

Milan Kundera,
The Book of Laughter and Forgetting

PART I
THE QUEST

Potrero Hill, San Francisco, 1980

Notice what you notice. – Allen Ginsberg
Remember to remember. – Henry Miller

Remember!

San Francisco, early 1980s

I am in graduate school at San Francisco State University's Center for Experimental and Interdisciplinary Art (CEIA)—big name, small department. The beauty of this modest conceptual art center is its flexibility and innovation. A dynamic faculty of working poets, filmmakers, photographers, multi-media artists, theorists, and devoted practitioners offer their latest experiments and push us to define our own.

"What is your mission?" my advisors ask me. "What is your quest?"

Louise Steinman and I had co-founded SO&SO&SO&SO in 1976 to experiment with making movement images, inspired by poets and post-modern dancers, our Bohemian roots and family stories, estate sale treasures, political events. These fragments from life had anchored our... well, it wasn't exactly a 'company.' "You're a storyteller," Louise said.

"I am?" I didn't know what I was, but we egged each other on and are both in the CEIA department for further interdisciplinary study.

I find an apartment on Potrero Hill, perched above a flower shop, kitty corner from a biker bar, the sunniest place in San Francisco. Mediterranean light hits walls at vivid angles. Painters use pastels. View, views, views of the bay from the bay window, sailboats, dim sum, city lights, language poets riffing on the heels of jazz and Zen, the sound of two hands clapping, women slapping tortilla rhythms in alleys in the Mission.

The mission.

The Environmental Art class is taught by Jock Reynolds,

the chairman of the CEIA department. We meet on the Tiburon Peninsula on weekends, at an old converted naval base partially owned and operated by the National Oceanic and Atmospheric Administration (NOAA), formerly occupied by a Miwok Indian village, Mexican land grant and cattle empire, cod-fishing company, and nautical school; then the Navy stretched a net across the bay to catch Japanese subs. Thirty-five acres of land have been transferred to San Francisco State—abandoned buildings, steel warehouses, cottages declared surplus, big concrete anchor blocks, old thick ropes, falling-down docks, dead-end dirt roads, eucalyptus and oak trees on the hillsides.

Jock, the visionary of the conversion plan, has us all chipping and painting walls and hauling out trash at the same time we make work, inspired by the history and remnants and nature of the place. We spend several weekends camped in a big boat hanger, throwing sleeping bags down in abandoned office corners, drinking beer and barbecuing chicken, going off to our various spots to dream and write and photograph and stage theatre.

I roll out of my sleeping bag one morning and am standing alone on the edge of the sea wall, early morning sunlight, water sparkling dance, queenly city in distance, impressionist visual trance. Then, without a sound, maybe a ripple, maybe two hundred yards away, an enormous black shark-like form slowly emerges from under the water, takes a peek, then eases back down and disappears below the surface, like it was never there. Gone.

I am frozen. I have no way to think about what I just saw. I know what I saw. I saw a nuclear submarine, a weapon of mass destruction. I don't know what that means, not really. I know I can't un-see it. I know it lives there, hiding out, below the surface. Now what?

What good is performance art?

The Berlin Wall is still up. The Cold War still divides body from soul. A Grade B actor, the Great Communicator, is now Commander-in-Chief of Star Wars. The Trickle- Down Theory is pissing on the Commonwealth. Rents are doubling. Harvey Milk, the first openly gay politician elected in California, on the Board of Supervisors, and his ally George Moscone, the progressive San Francisco Mayor whose neighborhood-centered vision for the city went against the will of centrist big developers, have both been assassinated. Then John Lennon. The AIDS Epidemic is spreading. Lights in the Castro are dimming.

MTV is imitating art is imitating MTV. Marshall McLuhan is right. The medium *is* the message. The avant-garde are doing Absolute Vodka ads. The cultural coup, the nuclear sub, it's all part of a pattern, a death cult leaving its mark, hidden behind celebrities, embedded in divisive language designed by the people who grow the economies, who plant messages through their media magicians. *1984* is around the corner. "Political language is designed to make lies sound truthful and murder respectable, and to give an appearance of solidity to pure wind," George Orwell writes in *Why I Write*.

What am I supposed to write?

I need to find a language to speak to this.

I decide to go to the source, to the origins of my memory, the nature and culture that surrounded me, to investigate how imagination is born in a place and rooted in time. I will compose with the memory data as a source of creative power.

That's my mission.

In Dada class I write a manifesto. *Remember!*

Then another manifesto. *Dance!*

Vision

For my thesis on "originality," I study with the John Collier, Jr., whose book, *Visual Anthropology: Photography as a Research Method*, was a landmark contribution to the science and art of observation, visual thinking, and cultural studies. He teaches us to go into the culture and follow our hunches, take pictures intuitively, immediately, without analyzing, then arrange the pictures in a sequence, like a storyboard, then write the ethnography from the arrangement of images.

My paper for John's class is a study of family documents. How was my memory constructed from this cultural record? I begin with the home movies Dad shot in Ohio in the '50s. He bought an 8mm movie camera with a bonus from the GI bill and began to document his world. I examine the images frame by frame to understand how family members naturally act, body language and character, where Dad posed everyone, what he valued.

His visual poetry is most eloquent in the early black and white footage—he records more in 1950-51 than he ever does again—when he is not habitually documenting the birthday parties and holidays, when he is free to visually explore the natural choreography between people, the seasons and landscapes of Ohio.

He pans across the farmlands to the barn, cuts to a close-up of Ira Quincy Rhoten, my grandfather, in his overcoat and snap brim hat, laughing with the two farm hands in plaid jackets, one with a cigarette, looking at the camera, like a Walker Evans photograph.

I see into my father's creative soul, his eye-heart, and into my own. I am free.

Mom is hanging up clothes in the narrow backyard of the

house in the working-class steel mill town on the Ohio River, where dad was raised, near the old Hungarian Hall and Uncle George's grocery store. Her apron has big pockets to hold the clothes pins. She smiles, does a funny 'go away' gesture, and the camera pans to Uncle Alex unrolling the clothesline. I dart in and out of the scene, a flash of curly hair, three years old.

I am alive in time.

MOTHER TONGUE
OHIO 1982

Back in Ohio I am at my parents' home, noticing the pictures I grew up with, pouring through the records—family albums, Bibles, letters. A Spirit stuck in in a time box in the attic jumps out at me. "Get me out of this hell hole." The words are scribbled on an envelope. "What is this?" I ask Mom. Her uncle Will had died in the state insane asylum where he was sent after a "nervous breakdown." Why didn't anyone get him out? He had served in WWI as a doctor, had seen the killing fields in Europe, had lost his beloved wife, the mother of his four boys.

What were the roots of this madness? What else is in the family closet?

Edith Banyas, from her memoir sketch, *Ancestors and Other Skeletons in the Closet*: "My cousin Bob, who always has a story, said my Dad and his Dad tried to trace the Rhoten lineage in Kentucky, but stopped when they found a Black family by that name. Josiah Rhoten, who came to Ohio from Kentucky, had slaves, or so my Dad said. Slaves often took their masters' names. I've been to the old Rhoten homestead many times and one of the relatives told me the spring house on the farm was a favorite gathering place of the first residents, the Indians."

The Indians hiding out in the hills around the county, escaping forced removal to reservations in Oklahoma, gathering at the spring. Who were their kin?

Josiah Rhoten owned human property before he came up from the South and settled in Highland County on Indian lands.

Josiah's "property" took the name *Rhoten* six generations ago in Kentucky, and my kin turned around and left that history behind.

Look, there's Mom wheeling the Buick around on the back roads, heading for Mowrystown, the village where she grew up in and where Grandma and Grandpa Rhoten live now. She is smoking a cigarette, and I'm sitting next to her, eight years old.

"I was born at home, attended by Dr. Chaney, because my mother Grace absolutely refused to have Doc Funk attend her. I don't blame her. He had some mysterious disease that turned his complexion an ominous blue-grey." She checks her lipstick in the rear-view mirror. "Despite that, he had three successive wives in his lifetime.

"You can't go home again." She's reading a book by Thomas Wolfe. We both open the side vents to let the smoke escape. Why? Why can't you go home again? That sounds horrible. Who's Thomas Wolfe anyway? But she just takes another puff, shifts gears, over a hill, down and around the bend, past the Fenwick brothers farm, the brick farmhouse. "The Fenwick brothers never married."

She stubs the cigarette out in the chrome ashtray and tells me about seeing *Gone With the Wind* for the first time. She and Dad were stationed in Charleston, South Carolina, during the war before Dad was shipped out. They lived on Tradd Street, in the old slave quarters behind the master house, around the corner from the old slave block.

"When Scarlet O'Hara shot the Yankee," she says, "everyone in the movie theatre stood up and cheered."

Mom wheels the silver Cadillac around the back roads of Southern Ohio; this one, Highway 28, is an old Shawnee Indian trail that leads to the village of Highland. She wants me to meet Catharine Ingersoll, her second cousin, an archivist, genealogist, and retired history teacher, who might help me on my quest.

Mom and Catharine share the same great-grandmother, Elizabeth Conard Edwards, a descendant of early Quaker colonists. Her daughter, Abigail, was Catherine's grandmother. Her son, William, was my mother's grandfather.

Catherine's picture window in a yellow kitchen, looking out on rustling corns fields, takes me to a place far away, yet familiar. She is shucking corn, sharing sorrows, a daughter lost to diphtheria. Each corn silk is attached to a single kernel. Every family has a corn field of sorrows. She walks to the maple hutch stuffed with old photographs and artifacts, opens a drawer, and pulls out a small book, the diary of Elizabeth Edwards, written during the Civil War, when she lived down the road in a red brick farmhouse on what is now known as *Underground Road*.

I hold the tiny book in my hand and turn the fragile page to the beginning of a history that is handwritten, pictures from a time and place, my great-great-grandmother's voice.

January 1, 1864

I arose this morning twelve minutes after 5—found it middling cold.

Thermometer ten degrees below zero, blowing strong.

No strangers here, but Adeline, the girls sewing at Maria's dress.

Men sitting around, too cold to work.

Quakers called fugitives from slavery *travelers and strangers*, a form of code.

FIRST STORYTELLERS

Carl Davis walks into the CEIA orientation meeting in his ugly fishing shoes and smiles, fresh from fishing in Alaska. He lives on Edith Alley in North Beach. His mom's name is Edith. My mom's name is Edith. Both Ediths played trumpets when they were young musicians. "Dada will kick you in the behind, and you will like it!" poet Tristin Tzara proclaims. "Life is more interesting than art!" We skip Dada class and go out into the California landscapes and start to explore the world together.

Carl leads me up to the old colonial city of San Cristobal de las Casas, in Chiapas, Mexico, in the Sierra Madres, the Mother Mountains, to the *Casa de Na Bolom*, the House of the Jaguar. An international group of artists and adventurers help run this cultural center, the home of photo journalist Gertrude Trude Blom. Targeted for her anti-fascist journalism, she fled Europe in 1939 and met archeologist and cartographer Franz Blom, who was riding horseback into the Selva Lacandóna, the jungles of southern Mexico that once held magnificent Mayan cities, centers of art, architecture, mathematics, temples. The cities were abandoned, swallowed up by the jungle, and the people dispersed into small bands to live for centuries as farmers and gatherers, traders and hunters, free of excess and imperial design.

The Bloms made many trips into the jungle to document the powerful cosmologies and cultures of the great disappearing forest cultures of the Lacandón Indians, the forest people who call themselves the True Mayans, the First Storytellers.

The Bloms bought the old villa in the '50s and opened the library, art collections, massive dining room table, extra rooms and cottages to visiting scholars, artists, travelers.

Their work to preserve the powerful wisdom being eroded by the destruction of the rain forests took form in photography, writing, activism, scholarship, direct engagement with the culture.

Chan K'in Viejo, spiritual leader and life-long friend of Trudi, said. "I have watched the Lacandónes who have given up their gods. They sit and look at paper they say was written by their Lord. But they never look up to see the works of Hahäkhyum—the sun, the stars, the sky."[1]

Na Bolom is an on-going respite for the Lacandón, who come and go from the compound. Both sexes have long straight hair, unisex tunics, smoke huge cigars, and emerge from the jungle wearing digital watches.

Near the ancient ruin of Palenque, the "spiritual homeland" of the Lacandón, Carl and I decide to marry. We choose April 15, 1984. Full Moon.

We didn't notice it was tax day. Big brother was off camera.

TALL WHEAT

In the dream, my sister Martha and I are flying over wheat fields. We zoom down and land, and we are running through a corridor of tall wheat into in a small town.

Tall Wheat is the name I give to my thesis performance work in 1984—the homage to Ohio and storytelling—home movies projected onto white tombstones, movement phrases, magic tricks, my animated super 8 film *Album*, anecdotes—the magical language of memory.

My director tells me to dip my fingers in flour and dust my hair white and knead bread while I speak the words of my great-great-grandmother, Elizabeth Edwards.

January 7
Snowed a little last night, a few degrees warmer, yet sleds running.
I went to help Susanne McCoy quilt a skirt. Had a nice time.
Abbie got a letter from Willie. He is at Camp Chase.
The girls went to meeting. No strangers today.

I imagine her worries about her son, William, a Union soldier, my great-grandfather.

I see her sitting at a little writing desk in her upstairs bedroom, looking out the window. She scans the bleak winter landscape, no one out on the road. The Strangers are safe to go. She signals to her son, who sets a lantern down beside the cistern, opens the lid, disappears inside and reappears with two figures. He points toward the next farm, and the figures disappear through the fields into the darkness. He shimmies down into the cistern again to fetch the water jug and soup pot, sweep out the room, get ready for more Strangers who come and go in the night.

Where did they go? Who are their great-great grandchildren?

ONLY WHAT IS

I am invited for an artist residency to collaborate with the staff at *Na Bolom*, a new venture for the cultural center and for me. I return to San Cristobal to the House of the Jaguar, and live in a cottage in the walled garden of the villa. Three delicious hot meals a day are served at a massive table in an elegant dining room. Gertrude Duby Blom sits at the head of the table in her Mexican dresses, red lipstick, turquoise jewelry. She only speaks Spanish and admonishes those who don't. She is in her eighties. Her passion is immense. Her mission is profound.

I'm not sure what I'm supposed to do, but am encouraged by Ken, the director, who wears velvet vests and silver bracelets, has piercing blue eyes, the presence of a man raised on a Minnesota farm, and currently guided by the teachings of Gurdjieff—*every breaking of the habit produces a change in the machine.* He tells me to take my time and hands me a joint.

I walk up the dirt road to the Mayan village of Chamula, hear chants to the Sun and Moon in the old church full of saints with swords puncturing different organs and body parts. I look at Mayan hieroglyphs in the library with the fireplace, read the ethnographies and cosmologies, gallop with Lucia, a horse woman, into the countryside where we are warned not to go into the cave because of the brujas, the witches. I watch a curtain in a window rise and fall in a whirlwind that passes through the zocalo, suspended, time bending. I buy glittery earrings and calla lilies at the market from women in deep blue shawls, with bare feet like thick clay, molded from the earth, long braids, elegant, strong. The Lacandón come and go from the compound.

"Learn the stories of your soul," poet Robert Bly says. "Memorize them and tell them." I hear his talk about storytelling right before I leave for Mexico.

"Tell a soul story," I direct the staff when we gather the first time. "A moment that changed you. Enter into the moment and describe it."

We listen, witness, paint images, reflect back, invent movement. For two months, I work one-on-one with each storyteller to create solos and duets, ensemble dance theatre, words, drumming, memory poetry. We perform at night in the blue tile courtyard, the library lit by the massive fireplace, a corner in the garden, the chapel filled with candles and saints and a grand piano played by Lorenzo, who evokes the conquest through his wild vocal classical search for a Muse. The stories are personal and dreamy, political and historic, musical and stylish.

In the enchantment of the old villa, a story form is born.

I name it *Soul Stories.*

The enchantment follows me back to San Francisco, where it has already reached Carl, and we create the dance that brings our child into the world. Our beautiful son looks like a tiny Mayan warlord.

We name him *Jack Quincy.*

Now the two Ediths have a grandson, and I have two children, a real boy, born in the Year of the Tiger, and a story form, born in the House of the Jaguar. And we all begin building a life together.

"No time for poetry," Jack Kerouac says, "only what is."

A BIGGER STORY
JULY, 1990

Fast-forward to the twenty-fifth Hillsboro High School Class Reunion, uptown at the Parker Hotel. There we are, a tribe of fellow time travelers, clinking our drinks, checking each other out, making the rounds, moving our memories out onto the dance floor. Aretha Franklin sings "Respect," and I'm swooping and dipping with Marva Curtis and ask her how she feels about being the only African American at the party. She keeps dancing, surveys the situation, and without an ounce of irony, looks straight back at me on the beat and says, "It was different for me."

Different. The word lands—kerplunk, on the downbeat—a shift, something breaks loose. Her wide-open smile, dancing, two histories intersecting on a beat, through a single word.

Then Benny, my first love, walks through the door, comes straight over, and pulls me close for a slow dance. He still smells like fresh hay right after it's cut, sweet and earthy. "You smell good," he says. "I never forgave your father for taking you away." He *had* liked me. "Hell yes," he says. I was thirteen when my family packed up and left Hillsboro, and I never said goodbye to Benny. I didn't know how. No one talked about feelings. "Is this closure?" he asks.

The first boy I ever loved is a forty-two-year-old man with a baseball cap, balding head, rough hands, strong body. Now he is removing the plastic wrapper from his cigar, licking it a few times, smiling, and lighting up. I laugh and take a deep whiff of the sweet smoke. "So satisfying to see you again," I say.

He smiles his cocky smile. "You have your ducks lined up," he says.

I'm not sure what ducks he means, but I feel his trust and it feels like pure good energy.

First love. *Trust.*

The day after the reunion my childhood friend, Connie Gordon and I set out to walk around the town, retracing our steps to Webster School. Her husband, Michael Kean, joins us. We stop outside our third-grade classroom window and recall Mrs. Mallory and the marching mothers who passed our window every day that year in the very spot we are standing. The memory is back, and we are standing in it again, on the other side of it. Then Michael steps in and opens the memory wider. He was doing graduate education study at Ohio State in 1970.

Michael Kean: "Connie and I were dating and she happened to mention this story about Hillsboro. I never knew anything about it and was really interested and had to do a term project for one of my courses with Charlie Glatt, my mentor. Lenora (Connie's mom) had articles. I went to the library, Cincinnati papers, background stuff, telling the story second-hand from newspaper accounts and magazine accounts, and I pieced it together."[2]

Michael recounts a *bigger story*, more fascinating than anything I'd ever heard, beginning with the county engineer, Philip Partridge, who sparks the action by torching the "colored school" in order to force integration two months after the *Brown* decision.

Apparently, Lenora did not find Michael's research fascinating in 1970 when he spoke up at a family dinner. Students shutting down campuses, battles over busing, hippies, Panthers, priests burning draft cards, paradigm shifts, conspiracy theories. Lenora was leery of his revelations, circa 1954 to 56, when she was the President of the PTA. When he shared his exposé of hometown history, the dinner table went silent, Michael remembers. *Dead silence.*

Pass the peas, please.

41

GONE MAD

I tuck the ducks from the reunion—*different, trust, bigger story, silence*—into the background of the next decade, the busy years of raising my son, burying my mother, running a movement arts studio, directing others to connect with their own dances, tell stories that help us heal, that boost the creative body-voice to a rich full volume. I teach and invent multi-media storytelling, but worry that I don't have the skills or know-how to protect my own child from the accelerated, alarming, unnerving, penetrating techno-stories swallowing imagination and childhood, stories with the War on Terror as a backdrop in a society "gone mad on war." Those were Dr. King's words, in 1967, before he was "neutralized."

Children are now "branded" in tidal waves of corporate advertising created by geniuses of the "creative class," who are keynote speakers at the art conferences I attend. I see teachers slipping real thinking in between federally-mandated testing, doling out pharmaceuticals like M&M's for ADHD and other "disorders," while violent video games designed to normalize killing are dumped into the market, "targeting" children. The virus is growing more virulent, spreading through media messages, hard to pin down. Military recruiters, like vultures, appear in my son's PE class, compliments of No Child Left Behind. War is normal. There's not much discussion.

Under the surface of the "talented and gifted program," there's Dr. Strangelove—"how to stop worrying and love the bomb"—in charge of foreign policy now. In this fog of war, I open the August 2001 issue of *The Sun* and read "Neighborhood Bully, Ramsey Clark and American Militarism," an interview by Derrick Jensen. Former Attorney General Ramsey Clark describes the nuclear submarine I saw and cannot forget, how it can destroy four hundred and eight centers of human population simultaneously. "What kind of mind would conceive of such a machine?" he says in the interview. "What justification could there be for its existence? What would be the meaning of daring to use it?"

THE SPIRIT OF HISTORY

Protests erupt around the world in the months leading up to the American invasion of Iraq, but the mainstream media, *The New York Times*, they're all cheerleading the war. The Pentagon, Hollywood, the gaming industry, Silicon Valley, they're all business partners now. Twenty-five thousand people have gathered at Riverfront Park in Portland for an anti-war protest in November, 2002. U.S. Congressman from Georgia, civil rights leader John Lewis, steps up to the podium. "Don't believe what they tell you in Washington," he thunders. "Be stirred by the spirit of history."

The marching mothers stepped into history to protect their children. My great-great-grandmother stood up to federal authority to change an evil system. The county engineer pushed the system to correct the imbalance. I am mulling this over— how I will speak to the war, to the lies that create war, to the addiction to war.

On March 19, 2003, U.S. airplanes begin bombing neighborhoods in Baghdad, near the mythical Garden of Eden, one of the oldest civilizations on earth. My son has just left for school. I look out the window at my beloved neighborhood and know at this very moment a mother in Iraq is looking out at her neighborhood that is being destroyed—children blown apart, husbands with dreams, who never came home, grandparents crushed by a collapsing world, the library of ancient wisdom blasted away. Mission accomplished, the American President says.

I book my ticket to Ohio to begin to write the story. I will return to find the people in my first protest memory, who faced the madness directly, with their bodies on the line. *Body first*, I spontaneously write on a little note and place it under the glass paper weight that magnifies the words. My body will be my intelligence source, help me retrieve what I felt but could not name, lead me to the sources that tell the bigger story. When memories intersect, things change.

YELLOW HELLO
PORTLAND, OREGON, MAY19, 2003

A muse the color of happiness flies into my future. Bigger than a story, this bird appears at the feeder. My son and I both notice the unusual yellow omen that hangs around a few days.

I am leaving for Ohio soon and have made arrangements to meet Philip Partridge, the ninety-three-year-old mystery man, to ask him, what was it all about? A partridge in a pear tree. A bird in the hand is worth two in the bush.

A yellow *hello*?

The day before I leave for Ohio, I find the bird in a basket upstairs near the wood stove. Here, inside? No marks of a struggle, simply gone, alive with feeling.

Who has died?

I make a phone call to check in on Philip Partridge, who has been ill. His son, Tom, the go-between, is surprised by my call, tells me his father died a half an hour earlier when I held the yellow bird, feathers still soft to the touch.

PART II
THE STORY

The Projector   Projection

Real life is only one kind of life.
There is also the life of the imagination.
E.B. White

CHARACTERS IN ORDER OF APPEARANCE

Voiced text from documents, cited texts, conversations, and interviews 2003-2012

Clara Alfrieda Goodrich, co-founder of African American Awareness Research Council

Eleanor Cumberland Curtis, daughter of Imogene Curtis

Elsie Steward Young, marching mother

Mrs. Mallory, teacher

John Banyas, my father, car dealer

Edith Banyas, my mother, housewife and storyteller

Pam Limes, childhood friend

Charlie Limes, Pam Limes' father, jeweler

Ditty Jackson, businessman

Lewis Goins, classmate

Junior Burns, Imogene Curtis' cousin and storyteller

Janet Limes, Pam Limes' mother

Connie Gordon, childhood friend and classmate

Lenora Gordon, Connie Gordon's mother

Philip Partridge, county engineer

Judge Richard Davis, county prosecutor

Elizabeth Partridge, Philip Partridge's wife and nurse

Imogene Curtis, marching mother

Gertrude Clemons Hudson, marching mother

Thurgood Marshall, General Counsel, NAACP LDF, later Supreme Court Justice

Paul Upp, school superintendent

Virginia Steward Harewood, daughter of Elsie Steward Young

Carolyn Steward Goins, daughter of Elsie Steward Young

Teresa Williams, daughter of Sally Williams

Joyce Clemons Kittrell, Plaintiff, daughter of Gertrude Clemons Hudson

Mr. Henry, school principal
Jane Henry, daughter of Mr. Henry
Mary Hackney, Quaker teacher
James Hapner, attorney for school board
Russell Carter, NAACP attorney for marching mothers
James McGee, NAACP attorney for marching mothers
Louie Robinson, *Jet Magazine* reporter
Judge John Druffle, federal district court judge, Cincinnati
Dr. R. E. Bushong, superintendent at Lima State Hospital
Tom Partridge, son of Philip Partridge
The Honorable Constance Baker Motley, NAACP attorney
for marching mothers
Dick Lukens, son of Doc Lukens, president of the Hillsboro
Board of Education, town veterinarian
Tamara Rogers, childhood friend and classmate
Mamie Till, mother of Emmet Till
Rosa Parks, activist
Lydia Lawson Burns, grandmother of Imogene Curtis
Anne Richter, sister of Philip Partridge
Jasper Seaton Hughes, grandfather of Philip Partridge
Allen Roberts and Martha Barnett, grandparents of Elsie
Stewart Young
Hannibal Hawk Williams, grandfather of Clara Alfrieda
Goodrich
Elizabeth and Robert Edwards, great-great grandparents of
Susan Banyas
William and Sarah Edwards, grandparents of Edith Banyas
Judge Potter Stewart, U.S. Court of Appeals judge, later
Supreme Court Justice
Doris Cumberland Woods, classmate

THIS IS THE BEGINNING
MAY, 2003, HILLSBORO, OHIO

Eleanor Curtis Cumberland, Elsie Steward Young,
Clara Alfrieda Goodrich, Trenton Street, 2003

Clara Alfrieda Goodrich answers the door and invites me into her white two-story house on Trenton Street to meet Elsie Steward Young and Eleanor Curtis Cumberland. Mrs. Goodrich sets a beautiful table, coffee cups, dessert plates, an apple pie. The three elegant women sitting before me have agreed to share their memories. Elise was one of the marching mothers outside my classroom window when I was eight years old. Eleanor's mother, Imogene Curtis, led the march that changed the educational landscape of my hometown. Clara Alfrieda Goodrich has graciously opened her home to me to support my curiosity. She is one of the leaders of the African American Awareness Research Council, a venue to preserve and showcase regional Black history. This is the beginning, this house, these women.

I didn't know then that the three women were to become my compass points and allies on this journey to find and tell a story that was buried in my memory field and tossed into the dump heap of history, at least on one side of town.

Elsie offers the prayer before we eat pie. I look around. Here we are, together. I feel accepted. I am not sure I have ever felt this. White culture is more suspicious and competitive. This is a quick, brief thought. I don't understand my tears, but there they are, a little fountain spilling forth. No one reacts. The women hold the space. I dab my eyes, turn on the tape recorder. How was it for you? What kept us apart?

MEMORY PLACE

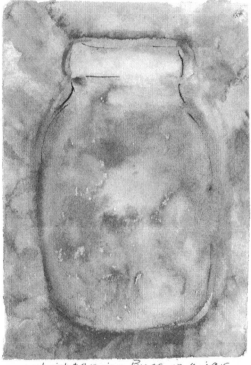

Lightening Bugs in a jar

Hillsboro is built on seven hills, like Rome,
which is why it's called Hillsboro.

HILLSBORO

WALNUT STREET
1955, WEBSTER ELEMENTARY SCHOOL

I am in Mrs. Mallory's class. She is reading us *Charlotte's Web* by E.B. White, and this is my favorite thing about third grade. A smart and sweet spider named Charlotte saves her best friend, Wilbur the pig, by weaving words into her web above Wilbur's pen. Some Pig, Humble, Radiant, Terrific.

"But Charlotte," said Wilbur, "I'm not terrific." "That doesn't make a particle of difference," replied Charlotte. "Not a particle. People believe almost anything they see in print. Does anybody here know how to spell 'terrific'?"

Negro women in shirtwaist dresses and their children walk back and forth outside the classroom window, carrying signs. Then they disappear. Then come back the next day. Back and forth on Walnut Street, every day, outside the window, all year, with signs.

Must Hillsboro Lag Behind the South?

Our Children Play Together, Why Can't They Learn Together?

Messages!

DANVILLE PIKE

Dad bought a Buick dealership in Hillsboro, Ohio in 1950, and our family settled into life on the outskirts of town. The prosperous middle class Eisenhower lifestyle we were entitled to was a direct legacy of Franklin Roosevelt's New Deal, my Dad said. GI benefits, support for farming, labor, education, small business, if you were white, and social security, unless you were a domestic or mother.

Mom stayed home to raise us four kids, *The Saturday Evening Post* on the coffee table a decade before *The Feminine Mystique* called into issue all that advertising about domestic bliss. Secrets were hiding on the top shelf of the linen closet in a shoebox from Shillito's marked *Later.* I couldn't reach the shelf.

Still, my mom said, "Those years on Danville Pike were my happiest."

I awaken to follow my plan to meet Jill Starbuck at Lukens' barn before dawn. We saddle Doc Lukens' ponies, head up the lane to the Pleasant Street. Clip clop, clip clop over to Vine to Walnut, clip clop up Walnut to the center of town. Trot down Main Street, canter down High Street, Queens of the Cowgirls!

Trot back to the barn, brush down the ponies, slink back to our houses. Jill's mom, Shirley, is upset and blames me for the whole thing, a total injustice. Mom seems nonchalant. The town is asleep. Why not show off?

PROSPERITY

Our ranch style house and the Limes' contemporary house are on either side of the Starbuck's colonial-style house. Pam Limes is my constant companion. Her parents, Janet and Charlie, are the Honeymooners of Danville Pike. They fight and crack jokes like Jackie Gleason and Audrey Meadows. My parents, Edith and John, are the sidekicks, except instead of tiny big city apartments and working class jobs, the foursome are moving up the ladder. Modern decor, a turquoise convertible, a Whirlpool washer, clothes on the line, Dad and Charlie drinking Schlitz beer, laughing in lawn chairs, in scenes backlit by optimism.

Banyas Buick Company is on High Street. The showroom is shiny, and the service department is grimy. My first job is to clean the stinky bathroom back there. I look up at the complicated bottom of a Buick on a hoist and wonder why it doesn't fall off onto Earl Bowen's head. He drives a Harley to work.

Dad's best friend, Charlie, owns Limes Jewelry on Main Street, the most modern store in town. Charlie is classy, a snappy dresser. He sits in the back of the store on a stool with a monocle in his eye, using tiny little tools to set gems, flicking his cigarette. Charlie fought at D-Day. He smokes a lot of cigarettes doing deals in the back room with his stockbroker.

Charlie can talk like Donald Duck, which is hilarious. He calls Dad the Big Banana. The two dynamos start the Hillsboro Business Association.

Dad: "We got a group together, started a development corporation. We were trying to get the local businesses to pay their employees better wages. Here was a guy working in the clothing store for twenty-five dollars a week.

"We had a program set up to get industry in here. We were trying to raise a hundred thousand dollars. Trying to raise a hundred thousand in Hillsboro in the '50s was a gigantic task. We got help from the State Development Corporation. DiSalle was Governor, a Democrat. We had to buy land–the city furnished water and sewer—and from that beginning, we went up to Detroit to bring Rotary Forms Press down from Detroit. They make forms, business forms. And Acro. They make parts, refrigerator parts."

Dad wanted to sell Buicks and Charlie wanted to sell diamonds, but people have to make a decent living first.

THE ONLY TELEPHONE

"Wilbur Jackson had the only telephone," Mrs. Goodrich says.

Ditty Jackson owned a car wash, raised hogs and tobacco he sold down in Ripley. Ditty was an enterprising landowner and bought a new car every year. But he couldn't buy blue chip stocks. The broker above the Merchant's Bank would not sell Ditty shares in Standard Oil or Proctor and Gamble. Black people were not supposed to get rich.

The two barbers in town were John Goodrich on 143½ Main Street, Alfrieda's husband, and Lang Young on Short Street, across from the court house. But John and Lang cut white hair only in their shops. The folks in their neighborhood came over to the houses for haircuts.

Lewis Goins: "Mr. Glenn was a jive time electrician. He ran in my granddad's group. My granddad had a group. He had a crew of bricklayers, electricians, and carpenters. They all worked together. Glenn Speech, Hard Rock, Junior Curtis, Harvey Ames, Jungle Jim, Howard Blair, Jimmy Day. They built any damn thing. My grandad died laying them stones on top of Merchants Bank. He was a helluva mason. Brick and block houses. Them guys made money back in the fifties. They had their own baseball league. Tom Stanforth found a photo of the team at an auction in Wilmington."

People Talk

Hillsboro, Ohio didn't act like Alabama on the surface; but at the Dean Martin and Jerry Lewis movies on Saturday, colored kids had to sit in the back of the Colony Theatre, off to one side. I ducked out during the newsreel to buy my *Good and Plenty* candy, clueless.

I ask a white person in Hillsboro now about segregation and hear that *this was the past and things have changed and they never knew about any Klan in Hillsboro.*

I ask a black person in Hillsboro now about segregation and hear that *the town is still prejudiced, hasn't changed much, and sure, out there on Mad River Road. That's where they met. The president of the Merchants and Farmers Bank was the Grand Duke Wizard.*

"Newt Winkle?" my Dad couldn't believe it. "Not old Newt. He always loaned me money. 'John, how much do you need?' Big heavy-set guy. He wore a long wool coat that came down to his ankles. You better check your sources, Susie."

Junior Burns: "The biggest Klansman in Hillsboro was the president of the Merchants National Bank uptown. Newt Winkle. He was the Grand Duke of the KKK. About six feet nine, weighed about three hundred pounds. I can see him walking down the street now with that pipe in his mouth. And the nicest fellow I ever wanted to meet. I was just a little kid. Dr. Fenner was in the Klan. Every time they had a Klan meeting, it was out on Dr. Fenner's farm. I know lots of them who would dance on Imogene's grave when Imogene died.

"I went to the post office one day when I got out of the service. Guy said to me, I can't think what his name was, 'What do you think of these colored people running up and down the streets behind that old Martin Luther King and picketing places where white folks sit in there and eat?' He said, 'We give em good jobs. We give em houses to live and everything. What more do they want? Someone ought to take and blow his brains out. That damn Kennedy up there, we should kill his ass too. Cause he'll have these niggers walking up on our porch and asking our white girls to date em.'

"I'm standing there with my mouth open. He said, 'Now what do you think about all that?' Well, there wasn't much I could say. I said, 'When I went into the service, it didn't say, we want you. It said, your country needs you. And I just took for granted that it was my country same as yours.' And he said, 'Yeah, that Martin Luther King should have his head blowed off.'

"And you know who else made that statement? J Edgar Hoover. Sitting up there head of the FBI. Presidents were so afraid of him. They wouldn't put him out of office 'cause he knew too much about all of them. So you see that went from the higher echelons to the lower echelons."

My friend Pam asks her mom, Janet, about Newt Winkle. "I wouldn't doubt it. He probably was in the Klan. Your grandfather was in the Klan. Don't tell Susie."

Pam and I are shocked. But in the 1920s, when Janet was a kid, the Klan was having a heyday in Ohio, advertising their picnics in the town paper, membership ahead of Mississippi's. I guess it was like joining the Elks, except weirder. I guess the Klan got too edgy for Pam's grandfather.

"Oh, he'd quit a long before then."

Then meaning 1954, the year of the fire.

Surveying the Situation

Mapping the territory, the prick of the compass is set in Connie Gordon's backyard. The three Gordon girls live kitty-corner from us. Connie, the oldest, is my age. There is a short hedge between our backyards. We go back and forth, back and forth, so much we make a hole in the hedge.

The Gordons are a Chevy family and the only Jewish family in town, so they don't have a Christmas tree. They go to a temple in Cincinnati, which I imagine is a building with very large pillars and long tables, like the ones Jesus knocked over when he was mad at the Philistines. Or maybe it was the Pharisees.

People say Christians are mad at Jews because the Jews killed Jesus. But I learn in Sunday school that Pontius Pilate killed Jesus, and he was a Roman, and Jesus was a Jew. Besides which, that happened so long time ago, I can't see why people are still mad about it. I don't think I ever was, but if I had ever been mad at Connie, it wouldn't have been because of Jesus.

If you accept Jesus as your personal savior, you are baptized and all your sins are washed away. Then you can eat of his body, the cracker (not as salty as Saltines) and drink of his blood, watery grape juice (not as strong as Welch's), from fairy glasses that slip into slots on a tinkling silver tray. As you do this, you remember that Jesus died for your sins, and then you are supposed to feel grateful.

Lenora, Connie's mom, is much stricter than my mom. One day, at Connie's house, I complain loudly. "I hate Michael Morris!" He was a pest and trouble maker and he locked my sister in a dog cage.

Lenore overhears me. "Never use that word again!" Her finger points at me.

I feel horrible. I didn't know the word *hate* was so bad.

THE FASHION SHOW

We go to Cincinnati twice a year to shop for outfits—fall for school outfits and spring for Easter outfits. Racks of fashions for all occasions, softness and yellow in spring, pleated tweed in fall, a full felt skirt with a poodle and a bright pink sweater to match the color in the poodle collar, a real show stopper.

Escalators go up and down, past mirrors within mirrors, sparkling jewels, and perfume bottles. Mom leads us up the grand staircase into the elegant lobby of the Netherland Plaza Hotel on Fountain Square. We ride the elevator up to the top of Carew Tower and see Cincinnati bustling to the edges of the Ohio River, bridges over to Kentucky, hills that go up to Mt. Adams where the artists live. After lunch at the Jewish Deli, Mom wheels the Buick up to Eden Park to the Cincinnati Art Museum, and we look at the Impressionists and naked Roman statues.

Mom smokes on the way home, fifty miles on curvy Route 50, shift, puff, pull over when Becky gets car sick, wheel into our driveway on Danville Pike, make dinner while we unwrap the tissue around each item and lay our outfits out on our pastel chenille bedspreads.

After supper, we do the dishes. Becky carries over. I wash and rinse. Martha dries and puts away. Then we disappear to the bedroom to get ready for The Fashion Show.

Mom plays the blonde piano by ear, a real talent. "In your Easter bonnet, with all the frills upon it…"

Martha's light gray suit with clean lines, black hat, white gloves, and black pumps suggests Manhattan. Susan is ready to board a boat from Boston in her tailored navy-blue suit with white trim, jaunty white hat, white gloves, and white shoes with a leather strap. Becky is the princess of cupcakes in a pink dress, dressy white sweater, lacy little hat, lace gloves, and shiny black shoes…. "Pardon me boys, is this the Chattanooga Choo Choo?"

The Pool

Pam and I fight in the morning, make up in the afternoon, and find a place in the field across the street to hide when the Russians come. Down the hill, through the field, is the town pool, the center of our summer universe, where I become a diver and synchronized swimmer.

Negro kids never swim in the pool, even though their moms are around the neighborhood. Rachael works for Janet. Elsie works for Martha. Lyda works for Lenore.

Eleanor Cumberland: "You had to buy a stock in the pool and pay so much maintenance fee a year. I think it was set up and designed that way, in my opinion, to keep black people out. But I don't think any blacks desired to be a member because it's always been a segregated pool, and because the blacks knew that they weren't welcome, so I don't think they desired to be a part of it, you know. I have a friend that has a membership, and she's tried I don't know how many times to get me to go to the pool with her—she's taken my grandchildren—but I just don't have any desire, I told her, 'I don't want to go up there and be stared at.' 'Oh Eleanor, they won't stare.' I say, 'You don't tell me.'"

Lewis Goins: "Somethin' else. You got all these suntan companies making millions and millions and millions of dollars from the ladies and men laying out there getting skin cancer from trying to get dark, but if we bumped into one of them, they would look at themselves and see if it rubbed off. That always blows my mind. But I just learned to deal with it."

Our moms were silent on the subject of the pool. Certain topics were never broached. Doors would open or close automatically—the pool, McGee's Coffee Shop, the dressing room at Shillito's. White middle-class prosperity boasted an unseen badge of privilege, like the silver brooch on the velvet tray at Limes Jewelry. It was shiny and beautiful, and I put it on and wore it politely.

THE FIRE
JULY 5, 1954

Felix Fields lived across the street from Lincoln School, where Lewis and Carolyn Goins live now. Felix and his wife heard the crackling of heat eating up books and desks and lesson plans, saw flames shooting out from the windows, and they called the fire department to report the fire at Lincoln School.

Lightning from an electrical storm illuminated the scene in flashes. In the shadows, Felix saw a white man drop a can of gasoline and run.

The firemen geared up—Dave Higham, Ledger McConnaughey, Orva Harshbarger, and Roger Faris. The fire engine screamed out of the brick station, left onto North High Street, right on North East Street. The Lincoln School sure as hell was on fire!

The sheriff suspected Gene Kittrell who was up to no good a lot of the time; and he went to Gene's house to investigate. The ladies in the neighborhood had their suspects—young boys full of devilment had started the fire. That white man Felix saw was a crazy racist.

Whites who clustered above the commotion wondered if an angry negro set the fire, revved up from the buzz on the recent *Brown* decision. *Life Magazine* had pictures of negro lawyers, standing on the steps in front of the Supreme Court, quoting the Constitution like pastors quote scripture.

A few folks worried about trouble brewing, stayed alert to car headlights coming in from Greenfield Pike in case it was the Klan.

THE COUNTY ENGINEER

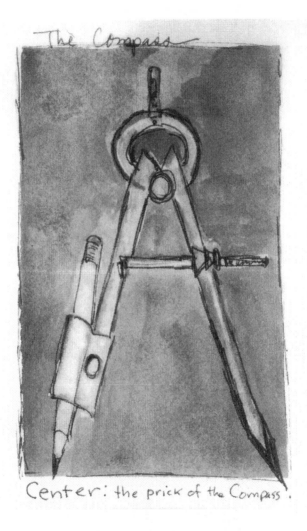

The Compass

Center: the prick of the Compass.

Why run and hide? –E.B. White

That Settled the Matter

Philip Partridge quotes, from his memoir,
If It Ain't Got That Swing

Philip Partridge, the Highland County Engineer, built bridges and laid pipes in '54 that are still fine sixty years later.

Philip Partridge: "Replacing thirty obsolete major bridges in four-and-a-half years—it was a tough job—lots of rivers and creeks, dozens of bridges, obsolete and in danger of collapse. If we tried to replace these one or two a year at contract prices, we would never make it.

"I devised a strategy of using the old bridge foundation walls as a core, and building new ones, wider, around them, and doing the structure ourselves. It worked well. We stayed within our budget, ran slightly over only once."

Philip Partridge was an athlete and a surveyor and knew how to level a playing field.

"When I came, department wages were the lowest in our nine-county area. When I left, they were the highest. When I came we had one black man on the payroll. By my second year as county engineer, we had four black employees. South Central Ohio was hardscrabble country, with a lot of poor people. Jobs were hard to get, and the county highway employment was good work. Maybe that was why a minor racial problem arose over work assignments. I had a before-work meeting in the barn the next day. The message was short. 'We are all part of a team. No racial discrimination will be tolerated.' That settled the matter."

The elegant brick Georgian style courthouse in the center of town would have been torn down were it not for his insistence on preservation, not demolition. The county engineer understood the power of a good design.

The courthouse stood at the crossroads between Main and High.

Businesses buzzed. There were four clothing stores, two shoe stores, a five and dime, meat market, movie theatre, stock yard and Saturday auctions, a lumber company that took up a city block, a pants factory, a bell foundry.

Stately homes wrapped around propriety and purpose stood on big lots with maples and oaks and sycamores. The status quo surrendered at the edges of town to ranch-style living with cocktails at five, Cheez Whiz on Ritz Crackers, and bridge clubs.

Tucked behind the major intersections in town, black culture carried on in funkier houses near Smoky Row, sweet singing on Sundays coming out of The New Hope Baptist Church, millions of moments between moms and kids, between lovers, between couples arguing, people vowing to make things better, between old people who'd seen it all and their self-absorbed teenage grandkids with their outfits and big ideas.

Two worlds, one county.

Philip Partridge: "Heaven help us. Segregated schools again. There was a degree of charm about the black kids' school, secluded on a back street in the shadows of tall trees. You would never see it unless you looked for it. Lincoln School."

The county engineer, poised and particular, was short on patience when it came to people trying to fold the same old attitudes into whole new possibilities. America was in motion.

70

This was a time for progress, true progress. This country had developed "the Bomb" and fantastic ad campaigns for Lucky Strikes. Why not apply all that intelligence and persuasive energy to developing the heart?

Philip: "How does a kid arrive at a resolution that shakes his world? Is there a sense of justice even in young children? I thought about things a great deal. Our well-read Aunt Ruby regaled us with tales of scoundrelism in our national past, not reported in the history books. The evidences of social and economic distress seemed to be always menacing the pursuit of happiness.

"I knew at an early age I was going to do something that would strike a blow at the way things were. I didn't know what. I didn't know when. But I had to be ready to send out ripples. As Martin Luther King later put it, 'creative tension.'

"Up through grade school, high school, college and twenty years of work, I never doubted the time and event would come."

With a fatalistic faith in the voices in his head and a sense of urgency as an agent of change, the county engineer went to work with a single tool, a match.

The Sign
July 5, 1954

Being a man of faith, the county engineer asked for a Sign. God knows he pushed the school board to consider conditions at Lincoln School—stairs out, third floor weak, playground equipment old and dated. Kids carrying firewood to school for heat and using outdated, hand-me-down books, he tells them. He knew all this because Alberta Jewett, who helped his wife, told him. Alberta's children went to Lincoln. All the colored kids did—from the time the school was built—in 1869 during Reconstruction—until now.

Safety? Integration?

The Hillsboro Board of Education listened to the concerns of the county engineer, lit their Lucky Strikes, and blew off *Brown*. They would get around to integrating later.

The school's namesake, Honest Abe Lincoln, was probably rolling over in his grave, stirred up again from all the betrayal. Was there no end to the Civil War? What are white people afraid of? Fear was packed into the bullet inside the gun aimed at the back of his head. Fear in the hand that gripped the gun, fear in the finger that pulled the trigger that blasted away the promise of Reconstruction. Hate was how it looked. Inside the bullet was fear.

Maybe Abraham Lincoln sent Philip Partridge the Sign.

Philip Partridge: "In the wee small hours of July 5, 1954, I popped wide awake and looked at the clock. Two o'clock. I quietly dressed and tiptoed downstairs.

"Armed with a can of gasoline, a bottle of oil and a clutch of newspapers, I kicked and struggled my way through a tangle of growth that choked an abandoned alley at the back of lots to the little cloistered school and up the steps. The door was locked. Nothing to do but smash the padlock for which purpose a crowbar did the job."

Spread the gas around.
Focus
Listen.
Now.... Ready.
Now, light the match. Get out.... Move!

The county engineer looks back from a distance. Flames flare up and out the windows. A *yes* shoots through his system.

He scrubs the gas smell out of his skin, sits at the kitchen table to quiet down. A few deep breaths later, he goes back to bed to rouse his wife.

The sirens, the electrical storm, her husband's passion for social justice are a bit much for the groggy Elizabeth Partridge. She is holding down a full-time job as a nurse, raising two boys. She knew he had strong feelings, but no idea he had this in mind.

Whatever comes out in the conversation between them, in the hour it takes the firemen to douse the fire and save Lincoln School, is part of the private universe between two souls who share a bed.

The Act and the Intent

The police were poking around Smoky Row looking for the suspect when Philip Partridge found out that a colored man was being accused of setting fire to the school. He phoned the county prosecutor, Richard Davis, and the county sheriff, F.F. Gustin, and asked them to meet him at the courthouse. Judge Davis remembers it was about eleven that night.

Judge Davis: "We had no indication of who had done it until Phil Partridge, who was a county employee with me and a friend of mine, called the sheriff and said he wanted to confess. We met in my office—the sheriff and I and Phil. There wasn't a big discussion. I looked at it from a prosecutor's perspective.

"The only things needed were the act and the intent. Fifty years ago, arson was not a probationary-type offense. If a person was convicted of arson, they had to spend a minimum of one year in the penitentiary. Today the prosecutors and defense attorneys often get together and negotiate down a charge. I never even considered that because I could have probably been disbarred. Law practice has changed. I was a one-man prosecutor. I made the sum of twenty-four hundred dollars a year. It wasn't for the money or glory. It was a job. I had a higher responsibility and a duty as the county prosecutor to prosecute the case. I don't regret what I did."

Philip Partridge: "My highway guys were shaken. Barney Young, Superintendent, greatest guy in the world. Later in the day my good friends, the Highland County Commissioners, called me into their office to tell me of their grief and shock at the news. And asked me to resign my position as Highland County Engineer. After a time of painful indecision, I knew I could not do it. I wrote the following letter, submitted it to the Commissioners, and walked out.

"Dear Sirs:

It is the right and duty of every citizen to take a firm stand for things he believes to be right. Where the need is great and the problem difficult, he must be prepared to make great sacrifices.

I was elected Highland County Engineer for a four year term on the Republican ticket. In accepting this office, I did not agree to surrender my rights and duties as a citizen.

My acts as a citizen have offended some people. I am not a habitual criminal, nor one likely to repeat the offense.

The need for a County Engineer in Highland County continues. There is no one who knows the road and bridge problems of Highland County as I do.

I should be derelict in my duties both as a citizen and as County Engineer if I should resign under these conditions.

Respectfully yours.

Philip Partridge"

"Next morning before daylight, there was an emphatic ring at our doorbell and my twelve-year-old son, Tom, ran tearfully upstairs to tell me there were men at the door with guns.

"They said they had a court order to take me to Lima State Hospital. I would be held for thirty days examination. They granted me time to finish shaving and eat breakfast. These done, I calmed my family's fears as best I could, and we were on our way."

EVERYDAY I HAD TO LIVE

Elizabeth Partridge didn't have time for town gossip. Her husband was serving his thirty-day evaluation sentence at the Lima State Hospital for the Criminally Insane, and she was the breadwinner now, facing a cool reception from those white-tiled kitchens.

Elizabeth Partridge: "I was working at the hospital and they tried to get me out of the hospital. They wanted to fire me. The superintendent said, 'No, she's one of the best nurses I have.' He wouldn't do it."

Elizabeth drove up in the Chevrolet to visit her husband every week, with her two boys, picnic basket of fried chicken, and extra oranges for the inmates, and made plans with Philip about their unknown future lives.

Philip Partridge: "Lima State Hospital for the Criminally Insane. Fascinating. There were about thirty-six men on Observation Ward 5. Mac and his buddy had lived a riotous life for over a year, the best hotels, wild gals, all from the spoils of service station robberies in Florida. Mac seemed to know all the ins and outs of the place. 'Lou, the guy that dispenses laundry?' A mild, quiet man. 'He killed his whole family, five children, his wife and her parents.'"

No cocktail hour with pretzel sticks for Elizabeth. She was dealing with teenage boys, sick people, Presbyterians, lawyers, letters from prison, loan officers, long distance phone calls to her people down in Tennessee.

Philip: "'See that fellow over there?' Mac said. He had an amicable grin on his face, a silly Robin Hood cap on his head. 'He was a brilliant student at a leading university. One day he took off all his clothes in class and stood naked. He was treated by a psychiatrist and returned to school. A few days later he again stripped before the whole class. He's been in here ever since. He'll do anything you tell him to. If you tell him to eat shit, he'll do it. He speaks three languages.'"

Elizabeth: "I never was afraid. The people I worked with and really knew well always treated me nice. I kept going to church and people at church were still friendly, most of them anyway. I didn't know if they weren't. I didn't pay any attention to it. I just got it in my head that if they acted like that, that was it. Because I wouldn't treat anybody like that, so if they wanted to treat me like that, it was their business."

Philip: "I tried to hide the tears that streaked down my cheeks and dripped in my stew. These lads were losers. Nobody gave a damn what happened to them."

Elizabeth: "I never thought about it being hard at the time. Day by day. Every day I had to live."

THE SCHOOL FIGHT

ignite

Make definite assertions. Avoid tame, colorless, hesitating, noncommittal language.
E.B. WHITE

THE *BROWN* PROMISE

If Philip Partridge was the spark that ignited the school fight, Imogene Curtis carried the torch. A visionary woman, Imogene was educated in the nearby village of Samantha in an integrated Quaker school and saw no reason for complacency on the issue of equal education. Her cousin, Junior Burns, said, "Imogene had the brain power."

Two days after the fire, on July 7, 1954, the school board stubbed out their Pall Malls in the ashtrays of the boardroom and concocted their scheme. Voters had passed a levy to upgrade the two "white" elementary schools, to be complete in two years. Then they would close Lincoln School and integrate. Meanwhile they would sink four thousand dollars into Lincoln to repair the fire damage, doll the place up with shiny new desks and bright paint, and let the colored kids stay put for now. Except now, with *Brown*, they had to legally cover their white butts.

For the first time in Hillsboro's checkered racial past, the board drew up school zones. White kids in one zone, colored kids in another zone. The zoning even went around individual houses so that the colored kids would continue to go to their school—for now. Superintendent Upp was quoted in the paper: "Segregation represents the spirit of the community."

Imogene Curtis knew that was a con, and the U.S. Constitution was on her side. But she needed her community to rally. She went next door on Baker Street to talk with her good friend, Gertrude Clemons.

Gertrude Clemons Hudson: "Imogene Curtis came to me and asked me, would I help her, that we would be together on this. And that's when we got the NAACP to come in. They came to Hillsboro from Dayton."

Imogene and Gertrude went door to door around Smoky Row, with the Constitution, some powerful attorneys from Dayton, and a growing NAACP membership on their side.

Then Imogene and Gertrude petitioned the school board in August, protesting the conditions at Lincoln and requesting immediate admittance into the white schools, warning of legal action if denied.

Then Imogene and Gertrude and three other Mothers clipped on their earrings, put on their high heels, and clicked on over to Webster School, my school, to register their combined twenty-two children for fall.

There would be no more colored schools and white schools. There would only be schools, where all children learn and grow and prosper. That was the *Brown* promise.

Dear Mrs. Curtis

"Your friendly letter has been a great help to my wife and I in our time of uncertainty.

We try not to think about what may lie ahead but just go about our daily affairs as though nothing has happened.

It must be that you have the same kind of leadership ability that Ted Lewis used so effectively in helping solve the school problem in Wilmington.

Many people seem to think I made a mistake. If so I earnestly hope that it has not harmed the cause of the colored people in Hillsboro or elsewhere.

Sincerely yours,

Philip H. Partridge"

September 10, 1954: The Hillsboro NAACP votes Imogene Curtis as the Vice President.

September 13, 1954: The Hillsboro School Board announces its zoning scheme and a letter goes out to all the parents:

"In accordance with the resolution of the Board of Education adopted September 13, 1954, children living within the city of Hillsboro will be assigned to and attend the elementary school building which their residence address determines...Webster School, west side of High street...Washington School, East Street north of Collins Ave... Lincoln School, Baker Street, Hill, Trenton.....

"The failure of any parent after September 16 to send his child to the proper school will result in the child being withdrawn from the school he is now attending.

Paul Upp, Superintendent of School."

The *Hillsboro Press Gazette* quotes the Superintendent:

"There has never been any great dissension here. Let us approach the matter in a dignified way. Let us pray about his thing, I say in all sincerity."

The *Cleveland Call and Post* editorial:

"The citizens of Hillsboro who are opposed to continuing this Jim Crow fester don't need to pray over it, they need to get fighting mad over it and go into the courts and do something about it right away."

September 19, 1954

"Dear Mrs. Curtis,

This is just a hasty note to thank you for your letter and to tell you the shabby trick the school board is trying to pull with its phony 'zoning' ordinance is only arousing more people to your support. The State NAACP, I understand, has been asked to make the Hillsboro fight its main business right now—and that's only the beginning.

Jean Tussey

Editor, Cleveland Call and Post"

Take Charge

Superintendent Paul Upp refused to meet with the mothers.

Dad: "Knowing Paul Upp, I can believe it. Somebody in that capacity should be fighting for the negro kids. It was a conflict that could have been avoided. He had it in his head that he didn't like blacks."

Imogene Curtis, Gertrude Clemons, Sally Williams, Seleika Dent, and Elsie Steward had it in their heads that Paul Upp would not push them around. They refused to send their kids to Lincoln and would show up every day at Webster with their children and their protest signs they made over at Imogene's house. MUST HILLSBORO LAG BEHIND THE SOUTH?

Elsie Steward Young: "I didn't have sense enough to be afraid. The women were the ones to take charge. The men were working. All the husbands were working, the ones that had husbands. I didn't have one at that time because my husband was passed.

"We'd meet in the center of town and walk down, snow or blow. It was quite a challenge. But we wanted the kids to have an education. The books they used at Lincoln had pages torn out. When they got to the seventh and eighth grades, they hadn't had fifth grade training and dropped out before high school. This is what we were fighting for. To get the same education.

"Any time there is a fire, it will damage the structure. I didn't want my kids down there, something falling or caving in. The upper part of the school could not be used. So they were all downstairs.

"There was not supposed to be anger. You don't get anything from being angry. If you're peaceful with people, you get a lot farther. Although they're keeping the children out of school, we are not going to do a lot of back talking. Stay in the focus of what you want, what you're doing. And that will get you farther than trying to push your weight, push yourself in.

"We'd all march down together. We were all friends. And the children would go up to the door to try to get in, and they wouldn't let them in. Some of the children, I think they resented the fact. Mine did. They hated to go up there and go to the school."

Virginia Steward Harewood: "As an eight- or nine-year-old, I felt like, 'Why does Mom keep taking us here? They don't want us. They're not going to let us in, but the Lincoln School was still open for business. We just didn't go. So the way I felt about it was, why would we do this? Day after day. If it had gone on two or three months, it wouldn't have been so bad, but this went on for two years. We walked in the rain or whatever it was, and I'm thinking, 'Why don't you let us go—there's kids there (at Lincoln)—until this thing gets straightened out.' Not realizing that if they had done that, we'd still be fightin' the fight."

Carolyn Steward Goins: "It bothered me because I was friends with some of the people. Billy Turner. See, we played together because we just lived down the street. Then we'd go to the march and they wouldn't let us in. That's crazy. It wasn't ever pleasant. We were going to walk and stand and wait. To see the other kids go into the school, and we knew they were not going to let us in. No, it wasn't pleasant at all."

TERRIFIC

I line up the cereal boxes on the kitchen table, choose Cheerios, tie my saddle shoes, cut through the back yard, through the hole in the hedge to pick up Connie, meet Tammy at the corner of Pleasant Street, pick up Sally, left on Vine to Sue Stanforth's, right on Walnut Street, step on a crack you break your mother's back, run to Harshbargers for penny candy, poke around down in the ravine by the school until the bell rings, test my speed, sit at my desk soaking up Mrs. Mallory's sweetness. She opens *Charlotte's Web*.

"Thanks," said Charlotte. "The meeting is now adjourned. I have a busy evening ahead of me. I've got to tear my web apart and write 'Terrific.'"

Outside the window, negro women and children appear and march past the classroom. They are calm, but something is wrong.

"A spider can produce several kinds of thread. She uses a dry, tough thread for foundation lines, and she uses a sticky thread for snare lines—the ones that catch and hold insects. Charlotte decided to use her dry thread for writing the new message. If I write the word 'Terrific' with sticky thread," she thought, "every bug that comes along will get stuck in it and spoil the effect."

WE WANT EQUAL EDUCATION FOR OUR CHILDREN

"When Lurvy arrived with breakfast, there was the handsome pig, and over him, woven neatly in block letters, was the word TERRIFIC. Another miracle."

Back and forth. Then they disappear.

How many Children		

Marching Mothers and Childrens

PREPARED BY: Teresa Williams DATE: Nov. 10, 2016
PROJECT TITLE: 1954

How many Children	#	
4	1	Sallie Williams – Deceased
1	2	Imojine Curtis – Deceased
1	3	Gertrude Clemons-Hudson – Deceased
1	4	Minnie Speech – Deceased
4	5	Silicka Deat – Deceased
2	6	Joanne Zimmerman – Deceased
4	7	Maxine Thomas – Deceased
1	8	Norma Rollins – Deceased
3	9	Francis Curtis – Deceased
3	10	Alberta Jewett – Deceased
2	11	Alberta Goins – Deceased
3	12	Dellia Cumberland – Deceased
1	13	Glea Clemons – Deceased
1	14	Roxie Clemons – Deceased
4	15	Elsie Young – Living
1	16	Zella Cumberland – Living
0	17	Rose Kiligore – Deceased
	18	Zora Cumberland – Deceased
	19	

I'D START MY DAY

Elsie: "I'd start my day around five-thirty. We'd start out about seven a.m., so we'd be there by eight-thirty. I'd go to work about nine-thirty after we marched. One day I'd go to Elberfelds, one day to Hottles, one day to Morris', one day to Duckwalls. Clean their house, wash their clothes, help them out. Everybody was very very good to me. We didn't talk about the school fight, didn't get into that."

Teresa Williams is the daughter of Sally Williams, one of the marching mothers. She wrote down the names of all the mothers and children, who at one time or another were involved in the school fight—eighteen mothers and thirty-six children.

Teresa: "There were a lot of kids in the school fight, but they had to drop out because people were threatening their families' jobs. Housekeepers and so on. Patty Goins. She had to come out because her mom worked for the Dickersons."

Joyce Clemons Kittrell: "We'd all meet in front of Miss Sally's. The parents would carry the signs. Then we would march up Walnut Street, all together, walking, talking, laughing. Sometimes a car would come by, say a few words to us like, 'What you niggers doing? Where you niggers going? Why don't you niggers go back where you belong?'"

Teresa: "We had to march all the time. And I remember there was a man that sat right across from the schoolhouse in his swing. Every morning. And they named him The Swing Man. We had to walk up and down there. We went into the hallways a couple of times, but they wouldn't let us stay."

Joyce: "Once you go through something like that, you never forget."

Teresa: "We were a little group that was going to hang together. We knew the conditions of the school. Most people didn't know. We could not mail stuff out from Hillsboro. Miss Imogene said, 'They're watching my mail.'"

Joyce: "Miss Imogene and my mom would get to talking. We were listening."

Elsie: "Get home after work about five. We didn't have washing machines. We had a washboard. Get clothes hung in the house in the wintertime to dry. I had five kids at home then. Sometimes I'd have beans cooked. Fried potatoes. Sometimes hamburger, wieners. We didn't have much meat. Sunday we had a big meal. Chicken, pork, whatever we could afford. Green beans we canned from the garden. Peaches in the summertime, the grocery put out boxes of peaches that were going bad, I'd get them to can. The kids would weed the garden, cut grass, we went together to pick berries, up at five a.m., by seven we were home with buckets full."

I Trusted Them

Motorcycle gangs vroomed by and gawked and yelled at the marching mothers. Cars crept into the neighborhood at night, bottles were thrown from the windows.

Gertrude: "I lost two jobs during the school fight. 'We won't be needing you anymore,' said the dentist's wife. I was cleaning her house. Her son is a dentist. He made my teeth. Lived near the armory. She didn't tell me she was firing me. She just told me she didn't need me anymore. I just didn't go back. I knew what it was. The Bolts had the shoe place. They told me they didn't need me. I went up to Wright Patterson." (Wright Patterson Air Force Base)

Support from the white community surfaced in secret.

Gertrude: "There was a woman who paid a hundred dollars for five of us to have a plate dinner in order to see King and his wife. And she said she didn't want her name told and no one ever told her name. King was giving speeches, and our NAACP gave him two-hundred-and-fifty dollars. He and her (Coretta Scott King) both were wonderful. He was on a crusade. They had an orchestra, but we didn't stay for that part."

The women drove home from Columbus, got up early the next day to take care of their families, march, go to work, and duke it out with white power, scapegoating the mothers.

Elsie: "We had to go to juvenile court because the school board was threatening us with jail time for not obeying the truancy laws. We went to Judge Rhoades to meet with him, Sister Lee and Gertrude and Roxie and Imogene and me.

"He said, 'I'll tell you ladies, you all send the children on back to school this year. And next year if they don't put them in, I'll head the fight.' He tried to reason with us."

Gertrude: "I spoke up and told the judge, 'Just let me get

my ironing done and I'll go to the jail.' It was comical in a way, and it was nerve-wracking in a way. I didn't care whether they were serious or not. I was thinking of the children. I knew if the judge put me in jail that the NAACP would get me out. I trusted them."

HE BROUGHT US THE CONSTITUTION

Beneath the radar of white power, a bee hive of activity took black attorneys to communities all over the state to hear redress, strategize, and communicate through church bulletins and the black press coming from Cleveland and Columbus. Dayton NAACP attorneys, Russell Carter and James McGee, young attorneys with law degrees from Harvard and Ohio State, were assigned to the Hillsboro case, supported by the best judicial civil rights minds in Ohio, in close contact with Thurgood Marshall at national headquarters, who bragged: "Those white crackers are going to get tired of having negro Lawyers beat 'em every day in court."

Civil rights activist and attorney, Juanita Jackson Mitchell, said of Thurgood Marshall, "He brought us the Constitution as a document like Moses brought his people the Ten Commandments."[3] Duke Ellington stopped his tour for a week to watch Marshall argue a case in Texas (*Sweatt v. Painter, 1950*). Ellington was denied accommodations in white hotels and restaurants where he played, but "I took the energy it takes to pout," Ellington said later, "and wrote some blues." The legal giant and his teams watched their rear-view mirrors as they drove around Dixie to take on Jim Crow through the courts.

Marshall led the team of tough-minded attorneys to the *Brown* victory, joining five school desegregation cases, from both sides of the Mason Dixon Line, before the Supreme Court from 1952 to '54 under one name, *Brown v. Board of Education Topeka, Kansas*. The victory pushed the national nervous system to high alert in a major turning point.

Thurgood Marshall: "It is at the elementary or primary education level that children, along with their acquisition of facts and figures, integrate and formulate basic ideas and attitudes about the society in which they live." The Dayton attorneys representing the marching mothers in federal district court were ready for battle.

Prima Facie

James Hapner was assigned to represent the Hillsboro Board of Education as the city solicitor of Hillsboro: "Segregated schools were outlawed in Ohio by the Ohio legislature about 1880. But outlawing them didn't end them. Before 1880, there was no provision for educating black people in Ohio. Ohio didn't ratify the Fourteenth Amendment till long after it was adopted—about 1876—about ten years after it was adopted by the other states.

"Southern Ohio's racial attitudes were different from those in Northern Ohio. Northern Ohio was strongly abolitionist, although the Underground Railroad ran through southern Ohio—it ran in this county. But you could be opposed to slavery without feeling that black people were equal to white people.

"We built our case on the fact that segregation was a temporary situation. As soon as these buildings were completed (renovations to the two "white" elementary schools), Lincoln School would close. Well, first we drew up districts to divide the city within the three elementary schools. It was obviously intended to maintain segregation. I drew it up and the school board adopted it. It was to try to put a *prima facie* basis for segregation, so we could say it wasn't on the basis of race. Of course it was."

Of course.

SKIN AND BONES

Webster Elementary, my school, was named after Daniel Webster, the silver-tongued orator and Massachusetts Senator who talked out of both sides of his mouth on the issue of slavery, a centrist. But he lost to the eccentric Abraham Lincoln. And then America's full-blown schizophrenia triggered a Civil War that cost six-hundred-and-twenty-thousand lives and set the stage for the Indian Wars, engineered to continue the effort to annihilate the North American Indigenous Tribes. Then Lincoln campaigned for the Fourteenth Amendment to guarantee equal protection for all citizens, then he was assassinated.

I always thought our school was named after the dictionary.

Mr. Henry was the principal at Webster when the marching mothers would arrive each day and send their children up to the side doors on Walnut Street to try to get in the school. Mr. Henry met them at the door and told them no. No desks, no chairs to sit on, no books, no place in the classroom.

I always wondered how Mr. Henry felt about the whole thing. His daughter, Jane, a year behind me in school, had straight blonde hair, cut in a pageboy, with straight bangs and always wore new shoes because Mr. Henry also owned Henry's Shoe Store, where I got my saddle shoes. Jane said their lives were topsy-turvy, that her Dad wanted to let the children into the school, but Superintendent Paul Upp told him he would be fired if he did. Her Dad got threatening letters from the KKK, hate mail. She said that it was a scary time.

I loved to stand on the x-ray machine, before they discovered that x-rays could give you cancer, and look through the viewfinder down at my bones in my feet.

Wow, bones are inside the body under the skin. Skin is just the *outside!*

TICKLED TO DEATH

Gertrude: "We home-schooled the children. The Quakers from Wilmington College came over to different houses to help. The home schools were called Kitchen Schools."

Imogene and Sally Williams monitored the kitchen schools, proctored the tests, were in touch with the Wilmington Quakers, kept attendance, managed the substitute teachers, kept the spirit of freedom alive.

Mary Hackney, a Quaker farm woman from Wilmington, came to Hillsboro once a week to teach in the Kitchen School: "We had to drive down every Monday. They were small houses you know in the black section. I was only there on Monday, and my assistant would teach the children the rest of the week. Her name was Miss Kilgore. I never had such a good substitute teacher and I mean, never. This lady wrote lesson plans to the T.

"Well, we had the first grade. There were about ten of them because they had never been in school. They were so bright and intelligent. I don't know if I've ever had a class like them. There was a Presbyterian minister, McCrackin was his name, down around Cincinnati somewhere. He came one day and said, 'Now I can help furnish?'

"I said, 'I wish I had a blackboard.'

"'Well, what else do you want?'

"And I said, 'We need about ten little chairs and a blackboard.' And so he brought it up that same day, and oh, the kids and I were just tickled to death.

"Then he said, 'Oh, Mrs. Hackney, now this next week, the assistant editor from Chicago for *Jet Magazine* is coming to Hillsboro and he'll be interviewing you when he comes.'

"Well, sure enough a big fine car drove up in front of Miss Kilgore's and he came in and interviewed me and had a write up in *Jet Magazine*."

ANTI-EVERYTHING

Jet Magazine reporter Louie Robinson: *"While the nation grabbed a ringside seat to watch Dixie wrestle with the giant bear of school integration, at least one northern city had hold on a frisky little integration cub of its own...*

"In contempt of the town's enforced school segregation, the Negro students and a few parents march nearly a mile each day to white Webster School to hear principal Harold Henry announce that 'there been no change' and deny them admittance. Then they return to three modest homes for classes in living rooms, kitchens and even bedrooms in what this small group of protestants have come to call Freedom Schools.

"Their desks are dinner tables and the tops of TV sets. Since the U.S. Supreme Court school desegregation order of May 17, 1954, the parents of these children have refused to allow them to attend the ancient, hard-to-heat Lincoln School, built for Negroes 96 years ago. The spanking brand-new Webster white school, built last year, bars them... Superintendent Paul Upp sought to wave away facts with a declaration. 'There is no trouble here.' But Mrs. Orval Curtis takes a suspicious view. 'They say they will integrate, but we don't know whether they will or not. They never did anything until we got after them.'

"As one white resident says, pointing out that hardly more than two Negroes in town are hired as anything but domestics: 'This town is anti-labor, anti-Negro, anti-Jew, anti-everything.'"[4]

Imogene claimed that the Kitchen Schools motivated the children more than attending Lincoln. They were building a movement. It was better to recognize the movement than to drop out of high school from lack of a good elementary education. It was better to keep moving forward toward the goals of good education than to keep quiet from the social pressure. Better to say *yes* to change than allow the white power system to go on with business as usual.

"I'd rather go to jail," said her husband Orval.

"Curtis, his wife, and fifteen other sets of parents were liable for prosecution for eight months last year for 'contributing to the delinquency of a minor,' with maximum penalties of one-thousand-dollar fines and a year in jail. Charges were not pressed,"[5] wrote Juanita Nelson, a graduate student from Ohio State University who went down to write about events in Hillsboro for *The Progressive.*

News was becoming national. My sweet little home town would have a hard time hiding out in the hills now, pretending to be a Norman Rockwell painting. The colors were intensifying, the shapes more angular and muscular, more active and luminous, more like a Jacob Lawrence painting.

THE CATCH

On the first day of the World Series, September 29, 1954, Elsie Steward was supposed to clean some white lady's house. Elsie sent her daughter, Geneva, instead.

Elsie: "And this lady said, 'Where is Elsie?' Geneva said, 'She had to go to Cincinnati to court.' The lady said, 'I don't know why your mom is in that. I thought she was a better woman than that.' Geneva said, 'I thought you were a better woman and would want kids to have the right kind of education.' She said, 'You shouldn't talk to an old woman like that.' Geneva said, 'You shouldn't talk about my mom like that.'"

Elsie: "We all went to court. Just the women, not the children. The lawyer for the Board was James Hapner. He was the one doing most of the talking. Our lawyers were Russell Carter and James McGee from Dayton."

The NAACP attorneys objected to the gerrymandering designed to maintain segregation, in direct violation of the Constitution. They knew how to forge a strong case for "equal protection" as guaranteed by the 14th Amendment's Equal Protection clause, without delay, could re-state and re-frame Thurgood Marshall's opinion in the *Brown* decision.

"Education cannot be separated from the social environment in which the child lives, He cannot attend separate schools and learn the meaning of equality."

James Hapner: "The District Court didn't buy our districting scheme, but it did accept that we were working in good faith to close the school (Lincoln School) and because of the confluence of the building program and the lawsuit, we didn't have room to operate."

District Court Judge John Druffel ruled in favor of the Hillsboro Board of Education on the grounds that the defendants had not been notified of the action. Another hearing on the matter was slated, but the Judge declined to act on the injunction, stating that the U.S. Supreme Court had not actually developed a "formula" for desegregation after *Brown I* and any decision at this time was "premature." The lower courts would wait for the Supreme Court to assign a remedy for desegregation.

He was stalling.

James Hapner, the victorious attorney, hurried home to watch the World Series. The marching mothers hurried home to fix supper. And New York Giants center fielder, Willie Mays made his legendary over-the-shoulder running grab—"the catch"—with his back to the infield from a long drive by Cleveland Indians' Vic Wertz.

The Giants won the game in the tenth inning, with Mays scoring the winning run.

Unfortunately for Ohio, the Giants swept the World Series.

Luckily for the ladies, the NAACP attorneys appealed Judge Druffel's decision, sending *Clemons v. Board of Education of Hillsboro, Ohio* to the United States Sixth Circuit Court of Appeals as the first test case for the *Brown* decision in the North.

Momentum was building.

CRAZY AND UPPITY

Do you think the author of this book is a nut?
He dares you to try to prove it. Or dreaming?
If so, don't wake him.

PHILIP PARTRIDGE

Awaiting Trial

After thirty days at Lima State Hospital for the Criminally Insane, Philip Partridge returned to Hillsboro to await trial, the court went through its judicial protocol, and he resided in the county jail, down the alley beside my dad's car lot. I used to creep by the windows. I could hear the inmates in there.

Philip Partridge: "My fellow inmates were interesting. A young fellow from Kentucky had 'accidentally' driven off with an old Ford, thinking it was his own. He gave me an expert haircut with a comb and razor blade.

"Three other young fellows were in for setting fire to an old house while drunk. They admitted guilt. They had been there for six months awaiting trial.

"A woman in the cell upstairs had been there as long as they had. She was invisible and completely isolated. Some of the cops made frequent visits to her cell.

"A curious phenomenon occurred. The day after I arrived, she was 'shipped out.' Hillsboro had become a focus of attention. City reporters were snooping around looking for stories.

"The jail was littered with abominable filth. Cigarette butts, match sticks, gum papers, dust and miscellaneous small trash. Meals were delivered to us on individual trays through a wall opening. The fare was the cheapest possible, lots of beans in ketchup, but edible.

"Why were these guys kept locked up? For six months? Highland County was a low-crime area. The Court docket couldn't have been that crowded. The Sheriff received a daily expense allowance for their care. Was he making a profit?"

CRAZY

Philip Partridge: "My distinguished uncle, Dr. Louis Lord, not a rich man, professor of Classics… arranged for lawyers, one from Cincinnati, one from Adams County next door. I must plead insanity, they assured me. Never. I said. But an Associated press story in the *Cincinnati Enquirer* said I would plead insanity. I phoned AP. I would not plead insanity. The story was false. But no retraction was ever published.

"I was questioned by five private psychiatrists and psychologists in the pre-trial interval. All gave me a clean bill of health. They seemed to agree with me. At Lima State Hospital for the Criminally Insane, I was brought before the head psychiatrist, a political appointee, for questioning. I had no secrets. I spoke up."

Philip: "The whole country was in a malaise, needed to be shook up—crime, alcoholism, drugs, suicides rampant, unemployment, divorce, insanity, frightful new weapons…"

Psychiatrist: "In Partridge we have a man who has superior general intelligence, but who has been rather poorly adjusted for the past several years. He is rigid, overly conscientious…"

Philip: "Outlawed segregated schools were just part of it."

Psychiatrist: "… and has for a long time been sympathetic to the underdog."

Philip: "When my trial came, it was completely out of my hands. 'God told him to do it,' my city attorney intoned, looking heavenward. I was never given a chance to state my case. My attorney pre-packaged me as a nut and I was not allowed to say one word at "my" trial. Insanity was the plea entered on my behalf and so it remains to this day in the County Court Records."

Psychiatrist: "When one notes that some of Partridge's behavior has been slightly irregular, that he has much paranoid ideation and that his judgment shows some impairment..."

Philip: "I was sentenced on two charges. Arson, one to fifteen. Breaking and entering, one to ten. Pronounced guilty and trundled off to the Ohio State Penitentiary."

Psychiatrist: "However, it is our opinion that he is still competent and legally sane."

The Defense's Thing

Tom Partridge, Philip's oldest son, was thirteen years old when his father faced prison:

"Pleading insanity. That was the defense's thing. The defense attorney convinced my mother, my mother was most distressed. We didn't know how long he'd be in jail, there were this horrible anger, feeling of bombardment, feeling of being besieged. It was very frightening. He kind of went along with it and then he regretted it very much. He told me that all his life. He was very sorry. Using this as a defense. He was such a strong and stubborn guy.

"He had an interest in school integration when he was city engineer in Wilmington. He knew a lot of the civil disobedience people—Fred Shuttlesworth, a lot of those people. The NAACP in Wilmington was all black then, and the city fathers didn't want him involved. A guy named Hamilton who ran a restaurant on the Wilmington campus—very bright black man, kind of a self-made guy who had a successful business—he and my dad became very good friends and somehow, with that association, he saw injustices in the way Hamilton was treated in the city, and I think, became more involved in civil rights. So when we came to Hillsboro, he already had an interest in things that needed to change. And when this came up... the school being cold... kids wearing winter clothes in school that had a wood stove... that was the straw that broke the camel's back.

"I remember very specifically that the lawyer talked to my mother at length... the way my dad reconstructed it later... yes, the lawyer convinced my mom to influence dad to plead insanity... because he regretted that very much. He was a very thoughtful person. Nothing was done out anger. Not at all. Yet the action itself was strong."

HANDCUFFS

Tom Partridge: "My Dad was not kept in jail during the trial. But I can remember him coming home and so forth and then I was in school and the trial was finishing up and all of a sudden I see

(*long pause*)

the sheriff's deputy in the doorway and he talked to the teacher and I could hear my name.

"I came out and my dad was out there and he took off his handcuffs. He hugged me and...

he said he was going to have to go away for a while and I told him I was proud of him.

(*long pause*)

"The sheriff was supposed to keep him in handcuffs. I guess they walked him out of the courthouse that way, but my dad told me later, the sheriff took him to the penitentiary; and even when he walked into the penitentiary he wouldn't put handcuffs on him.

(*pause*)

"The guards did when he came in there, he said, but the sheriff wouldn't do it.

"You know, I've never talked about this."

It's Hard to Get a Date if You're a Communist

I hear the word *penitentiary* and see a dark hard hell. Dad knows people who got sent to the pen for running numbers. Why is it a crime to run around with numbers? That's where they're sending the county engineer. Crazy.

Tom Partridge: "I was called a Communist. Even worse than being a nigger lover was to be a communist. There was a lot of fear in the country left over from the McCarthy days. And in a small town like this, a significant number of people here were affected.

"The FBI was looking at my dad early on. I'm sure there's a file on him. I don't know what's in court and stuff, but he said people were listening to us. I have no doubt about it. Right-wing screwballs are always digging around. You know what I mean? It was the Commie threat that J. Edgar Hoover talked about. Anyone involved in civil rights was obviously a Communist.

"I have no doubt that our telephones were bugged. Things were not as sophisticated. My dad would say, 'Be careful what you say.' I could hear stuff, squeaks and stuff on the phone. I really didn't have anything to hide. We had a nut running the FBI who thought we were a national security problem.

"I got beat up a couple of times by white kids. One time a black kid jumped me, but someone broke that up. I considered him a friend, but he was really upset that my father had burned his school. It was just the oddest thing, just the weirdest thing. I was just as confused as they were. I didn't know what the hell was going on. I did have some friends I didn't know I had. I'm thinking of Richard Blankenship, Bill Robinson, a tough farm kid, got me over the hump, just very protective without ever saying a thing.

"My Mom, I don't know how she did it. I swear. People threw garbage on our front yard. I used to clean the garbage up so my mom wouldn't see it. I cleaned a lot of garbage up.

"It's hard to get a date if you're a Communist. I didn't have much going for me anyway. I was this little guy. People whisper stuff. You walk up to a group and they just disappear.

"That was a big one, that was a biggie."

CROSS BURNING

Superintendent Paul Upp was beginning to worry about all the bad press. Even Governor Frank Lausche issued a statement: "My belief is firm that in a few school districts of Ohio, a wrong is being committed on Negro children, and I express hope that these wrongs would be rectified."

Paul Upp put pressure on Ray Paul, a high-ranking board member of the Cincinnati chapter of the NAACP. "Stop this thing," the Hillsboro Superintendent demanded. "You have the power to stop or continue the dispute."

Ray Paul said, "I might be willing to go along if I found one white youngster in Lincoln School."

"The NAACP has only caused trouble by trying to rush things," the Hillsboro Board of Education President, Doc Lukens, said in a newspaper article.

His son, Dick Lukens, two years behind me in school, said, "He received a lot of hate mail from down south, real racists, Klan who found out about it through the national news. Calling him a nigger lover, he ought to be shot. Mrs. Curtis was on his butt. I don't remember my dad being a racist. It just wasn't who he was. I do remember him saying in retrospect that he thought as a young professional family man it was his duty to serve the community and he wished someone would shoot him if he ever stepped forward to take a job like that again."

"There has never been any race violence in Hillsboro," *The Cincinnati Enquirer* wrote in an article about the school fight, indicating the women were out of line. But if the *Enquirer* had investigated inside the black community, someone might have pointed out the garage behind Hammond's Grocery.

Lewis Goins: "Old Man Hammond. My Grandad built that cinderblock garage. Mr. Hammond used to work with my Grandad, used to drink with my Grandad. He was in the Klan."

That's where they made the cross that was burned across from Gertrude's house.

Judy Clemons, Gertrude's daughter said, "I remember waking up and seeing that cross burning." Gertrude told her daughters, Judy and Joyce, "They can burn the cross, but unless they burn us, we're going to keep marching."

Tamara Rogers' family lived in the house that the Partridge family moved into later, near Smoky Row.

Tamara: "The house was built in the 1800s. A former inn, it was open and creaky. Voices danced off the walls. One morning I awoke to a wave of anxious voices. In the neighbors' front yard, I saw a cross burning. It was a cloudy, damp spring day, and the valiant forsythia bushes were dotted with yellow blossoms. Why is there a cross out there, and why does it look as if it were burnt by fire? Mother gave me a brief and honest explanation, but I only grasped a small bit of it. Nevertheless, this event struck me—like lightning on the soul—with the idea that people do bad things to others. It was a moment that I have never forgotten: that first revelation of cruelty. I still feel the burn in my chest."[6]

DAD BURN YOUR HIDE

The smoke from the cross burning drifted up the hill and across the street to the stately mansion perched on High Street, the location for Junior Burns' childhood memory.

Wesley Junior Burns: "Doc Larkin lived in that big yellow house right across from Billy Turners—he was a WWI Doctor—and he'd always say to me, 'Your granddaddy stole my girlfriend.' I was only ten years old, polishing his nice marble table, polishing his silver where he served his drinks. Him and Daisy Larkin. Had me chase the Pence kids out of her flower garden. I said to my dad, 'What is Doc Larkin talking about?'

"Well, Ollie Nun was engaged to be married to Doc Larkin the next month. And he hired Grandpa Ike to go over there and work on the farm. And Ike seen Ollie. And Ollie seen Ike. And they took off in the buggy. And Grandpa Ike married Grandma Ollie. They had eight children up on High Top. Four boys and four girls.

"Ike went to the mailbox and there was a big package hanging from it. He called her Oi. He said 'Oi, we got some mail.' They opened it up and it was a record. You know, the old 78 records. They started playing it. And the name of the record was "Run Nigger Run." That's the truth, God strike me dead. Grandpa Ike was six-feet-nine and weighed about three hundred pounds, solid muscle, not fat. He hitched up his two horses, Bob and Argen—he had a two-horse buggy like you see on TV, with glass lanterns on the side—and went down to Samantha. A white man down there named Squid Caldwell told me this. He said Big Ike went in there and his big shadow knocked the sun out. Big Ike didn't curse, didn't curse at all. He walked in there and said, 'Now gentlemen, I know some of you sent this record to me and Oi up there on High Top. But dad burn your hide, I'm going to tell you right now, if you come up there and bother me, I'm going to bury you there.' He turned right around, got in his buggy, and rode away."

HER NAME WAS MOTLEY

The marching mothers continued to hit the streets with their protest signs, ironed and cleaned houses for the white women, took care of their own families, and home-schooled the children. The Hillsboro Board of Education huddled in the boardroom, ruminating on various forms of delay. The Klan held their secret meetings to drum up hate. And Thurgood Marshall perused the playing field, and saw a good chance for another victory.

Gertrude Clemons Hudson: "Then Thurgood Marshall got in. He had a lawyer. Her name was Motley. And she would come see what we were doing and help us out."

Fresh out Columbia Law School, Constance Baker Motley walked into the cramped NY City headquarters of the NAACP Legal Defense Fund (LDF), and Thurgood Marshall "hired me on the spot," she wrote. "Over the years, he told me about every successful African-American woman he encountered. Marshall was born and grew up at a time when nobody had to tell him that African American males were on the bottom rung of the ladder in every conceivable professional endeavor and that African American women were not even on the ladder."

Marshall introduced her to Charles Hamilton Houston, Dean of Howard Law School, who trained the first generation of Civil Rights lawyers, mentored Marshall, and was the architect of the legal campaign to end segregation. "Marshall wanted me to learn from the master. Houston had a notebook in which every question he was going to ask was written out. His advice to me was: 'Never ask a question which you have not previously considered.'[7]

"In its cases, LDF always emphasized that we sought civil equality in the public domain, guaranteed by the Fourteenth Amendment's *equal protection* clause…. Thurgood, a black Southerner, understood whites' fear of intermarriage as well as he understood anything… what used to be called 'the mongrelization of the races.' We wanted whites to understand that we were seeking civil equality—the right to vote, the right to go to public schools, the right to travel free from state-enforced segregation, and the right to be free from state-sanctioned lynching and police assaults based on race…. The Court's decision in *Brown*—sweeping, straightforward, simply written, and unanimous—gained the status of a Magna Carta in the black community… laymen saw it as a mandate to end all segregation… a new vision of the Constitution among grass roots Blacks.

"My feeling after *Brown* was often one of depression. Awaiting the Court's 1954 decision had been about all the stress we could bear. I kept thinking: How will we manage? The staff was small, our funds meager, our plans sketchy; thousands of school districts were involved."[8]

After Philip Partridge lit the fire and the school fight lit up Hillsboro, Marshall dispatched one of his chief strategists to assist the Ohio team. Constance Baker Motley packed her briefcase and headed to Ohio.

1955

The Crossroads

I am a member of a party of one.
And I live in an age of fear.
E.B. WHITE

January

Philip Partridge : "Ohio State Penitentiary, the maximum security prison for hard-core incorrigibles; another education. Eight floors of cells side by side, eight by eight by eight feet, fold-away wall beds, four men to a cell, sink and toilet bowl at end.

"Daily we all marched in close formation to the huge dining room. Two separate battalions, one all white, one all black. I dropped out of the white battalion and fell in with the black battalion for a few days. One of the older guards said, 'Don't do that.'

"I did it one more time to make my point, then quit. I had no desire to incite trouble."

The Pentagon announces plans to develop ICBMs, long-range delivery systems for nuclear weapons.

FEBRUARY

Eisenhower says his appointment of Earl Warren as Chief Justice to the Supreme Court was "the biggest damn fool mistake I ever made." Warren had brokered the unanimous *Brown* decision nine months earlier, but Eisenhower can't commit. Without his willingness to steer the complex course of integration, fear and mob violence escalate.

On February 12, Eisenhower sends the first U.S. advisors to South Vietnam.

MARCH

Philip Partridge is transferred to Roseville Honor Prison, where he celebrates his forty-fourth birthday on March 29, 1955.

Philip P: "The black inmates; I will never forget them. There was Burr. Two flashing gold teeth, enchanting laughter. It would make a sick person well just to hear him. One day there were hot words. His eyes flashed. His face was white with rage. Did you ever see a brown man turn white?"

April

I get my first polio shot and learn about the Iron Lung and the Iron Curtain. My Hungarian grandmother came from behind the Iron Curtain before they put it up. She gets desperate letters from her family back in the old country. "Send food, send money!"

"Ach, the old country," Grandma said, "I never want to go back."

Soviet tanks roll into Budapest. The Prime Minister of Hungary, Imre Nagy, goes on Radio Free Kossuth and pleads to the free world for help. The UN watches. America does nothing. The radio goes silent.

When I drink a bottle of Coca-Cola, I think about Molotov cocktails and the brave Hungarians and the Hungarian Revolution!

MAY

Philip Partridge: "The big job was building a new prison dining room building. I was pretty sure we could do it in three months. One of the guys had a classy radio with lively music. We cleaned up the truckloads of dumped salvage brickwork, poured foundations, laid up the brick walls, installed windows and doors, roofed it and by May it was done."

Brown II is handed down by the Supreme Court, directing the states to "eliminate vestiges of segregation root and branch" with "all deliberate speed."

Translation: Take your time; the feds are more or less hands-off.

Three hundred thousand people have now joined White Citizen's Council groups, the black tie version of the KKK. They demand organized resistance to the U.S. government. Mississippi Senator James Eastland thunders at a rally: "When in the course of human events it becomes necessary to abolish the negro race, proper methods should be used. Among these are guns, bows and arrows, slingshots and knives... All whites are created equal with certain rights, among these are life, liberty and the pursuit of dead niggers."

JUNE

Philip Partridge: "There was Middlebrooks. Police had broken down the door of his apartment in Cleveland where he slept with a white woman. He fired a revolver at them, minor injury. Three times he had come up for parole; three times turned down. He was doing the last five years of his maximum sentence—twenty-five years. Compare this with a Number One hit man for Murder, Inc. who went out on his first try after donating one thousand dollars to the Catholic Church. According to prison legend."

July

Disneyland opens. Annette Funicello is my favorite Mouseketeer.

Philip Partridge: "There was Charles, the black man's Jack Benny. He was fun to work with. He'd been shot escaping from a robbery... There was Crawford. He kept asking me, "Can I work for you after we get out?" I would have been delighted to have him and all of them, the whole crew."

AUGUST

Philip Partridge is released from prison and returns to Hillsboro in time for the birthday of his oldest son, Tom, who turns fourteen.

Mamie Till had warned her only son, fourteen-year-old Emmett, to mind his manners when she put him on the train from Chicago to Money, Mississippi, to spend the summer with his great-uncle. But the high-spirited Emmett didn't understand the dark southern mood swing after the *Brown* decision.

On August 31, local authorities pulled the body of Emmett Till from the bottom of the Tallahatchie River. He had been shot through the head, one eye gouged out, and a seventy-five-pound cotton gin fan was wired to his neck. Mamie Till left the casket open, with no makeup, to show America what hate looks like.

October
FEDERAL COURT HOUSE, CINCINNATI

Judges Potter Stewart, Shakleford Miller, Jr., and presiding Judge, Florence Allen to hear *Clemons v. Board of Education of Hillsboro, Ohio*

Presiding Judge of the Sixth Circuit Court of Appeals, Florence Allen, wears her hair in two side swirls, and to add to this dignified feminine flair, gold earrings that accent her black robes. She hits the gavel with a light, crisp confidence.

Gertrude Clemons arrives in court in a white shirtwaist dress with a v-neck cut and wide collar, white earrings, black heels, a white purse. Her daughter, Joyce, the Plaintiff, is wearing a yellow dress with black patent leather shoes and lacy socks.

James Hapner, the freckle-face city solicitor with dark framed glasses, who is representing the Hillsboro school board, walks into court in shiny black Florsheims and a gray pin-striped suit.

His opponent arrives through the court doors.

James Hapner: "Constance Baker Motley. She was tall and slender and well-spoken, a good attorney. The burden of proof is on the appellate. They have to show that the lower court is wrong. We argued that we were not a segregated school system—the high school and junior high were integrated—and we were on record to close the segregated elementary school.

"*Brown II* had just come out, and we argued that we were proceeding 'with all deliberate speed.' Unfortunately, the panel that heard the case—unfortunately from the position of a lawyer—was presided over by Justice Florence Allen, the first lady to serve on the Supreme Court of Ohio. President Roosevelt had appointed her to the Sixth Circuit Court of Appeals."

Constance Baker Motley's signature courtroom style was to indulge witnesses, appearing to believe their testimony, then step onto the runway, and deliver.

"Ms. Motley argued that, in fact, we had been illegal for seventy years, and wanting to continue for two more years was an abuse of power and serious injury to the Plaintiff."

The Court agrees with Ms. Motley.

Constance Baker Motley goes on to win nine of the ten cases she argues before the Supreme Court. But her style seasons over time.

Then, in 1955, the young attorney with cropped hair swept to one side, skin the color of West Indies Mahogany, wearing a tailored black dress, white pearls, white pearl earrings, and black high heels, is just hitting her stride.

November

I spend hours at Lukens' barn, brushing the pony's dusty fur and tough mane.

I put my cheek next to his soft nose and inhale. I look into his big deep eyes, and fall in love with pony smells and the barn and the little lane down to the barn. I fall in love with life.

Mrs. Mallory reads on.

"Mrs. Arable Fidgeted. "Fern says the animals talk to each other. Dr. Dorian, do you believe animals talk?"

"If Fern says that the animals in Zuckerman's barn talk, I'm quite ready to believe her. Perhaps if people talked less, animals would talk more. People are incessant talkers—I can give you my word on that."

Mrs. Mallory has a big sand table by the window where we make Pilgrims and Indians with twigs, Popsicle sticks, construction paper and acorns. Outside the window, negro women and children march with signs. Up and down the street, they quietly pass our window. Then they leave. Then they show up again the next day. Every day, even in the rain, even in the snow.

December

Near the close of 1955, Albert Einstein, James Dean, and Charlie Parker have left the planet; Whoopie Goldberg, Bill Gates, and Mark David Chapman have arrived.

Nobody is awarded the Nobel Peace Prize.

On December 1, 1955, supported by a well-organized network, Rosa Parks remained seated. "When the white driver stepped toward us, when he waved his hand and ordered us up and out of our seats, I felt a determination cover my body like a quilt on a winter night.

"The bus driver said, 'Well, if you don't stand up, I'm going to have to call the police and have you arrested.'

"I replied, 'You may do that.'"

SPIRITS OF HISTORY

Gertrude Clemons Hudson: "My grandmother, who was in slavery, was Indian, a Cherokee.

She escaped and came from somewhere around Sardinia. She was probably from Kentucky.

Her name was Elizabeth Hurley. My whole family has always been a fighting family.

Not for fame, but for good, for equal rights. I never let nothing frighten me or scare me."

Imogene Louise Curtis

'Led Hillsboro Lincoln School DeSegregation Fight 1954

JOHNNY ON THE SPOT

Eleanor Curtis Cumberland:
"I knew my mom was a humanitarian. She was an *involved* person. A strict mother, but loving. Involved in her church. If someone came along and said, 'we're having trouble over here, will you go with us' or 'they're not treating us right, will you go with us,' she was Johnny-on-the-spot to go. White people came to her. Black people. You want to see Imogene Curtis. She'll know where to get you some help."

Junior Burns: "Imogene was living on Mary Jones' farm in a house over in the fields across from the graveyard. She was raised by her grandmother, Lidia Lawson Burns. Imogene had the know-how, you know. She was always that way, from when she was a kid on up. If something was going on, she had to know about it. She had to know why and how and when. She always was ambitious. Her grandmother was that way. Aunt Lid was that way."

Lydia Lawson Burns, center — Imogene Curtis, far right
"Aunt Lid, she was smart. She was born into slavery. She always said she shook hands with Abraham Lincoln when she was six years old. Aunt Lid told stories. Some of them was bitter and some was good. She said they was like a bonded family. After slavery was over, they didn't know what to do. It was like pushing your children out the door and saying you can't be around now. I can't be having you around no more. She said that's just the way it was. It was sad. It was scary for both sides. They didn't know how to operate without the other.

"I imagine Aunt Lid was about a hundred and ten when she died. She'd walk from High Top to Samantha and get what she wanted, her little knick-knacks and goodies and carry it clear back up in a gunny sack from Samantha. Aunt Lid went to the Quaker Church in Samantha. Quakers were liberal. I think that did influence Imogene. Aunt Lid was way ahead of her time, way ahead of her time. It was like a gift. I never heard anyone say she had enemies. Everybody knew Lidia Lawson Burns."

Jasper Seaton Hughes,
You Will Not Have To Go To War

When they were children, Philip Partridge and his sister, Ann, went to live with their grandfather in the summers. Ann Richter: "Our grandfather had an apple orchard here in Holland, Michigan. When he was called to the Civil War, he packed his valise—toothbrush and shaving kit and whatever—and sat in the living room and waited for the sheriff to come and arrest him. And the sheriff came and he said, 'Now what is this, Hughes?' My grandfather's name was Jasper Seaton Hughes. And he told the sheriff he was studying for the ministry and he could not kill a man and that he would not be able to go to war. And so the sheriff said, 'Jasper Seaton Hughes, you will not have to go to war.' Our grandfather also baptized the first black woman in the church that he preached in. He lost his pulpit because he baptized a black person. I'm sure it had a strong influence on my brother, Philip."

WE HAD EVERYTHING WE NEEDED

Elsie Young: "This is my grandfather, Allen Roberts, and my grandmother, Martha Barnett. He was born in Virginia before the Civil War. His brother, Andrew, married Ellen Hemmings. She was the daughter of Sally Hemmings and Thomas Jefferson. We don't know what's in anybody's background. Those were slave times. My great-grandfather, Giles Roberts, was born in Virginia. He was probably enslaved. They moved up to Pike County after the Civil War and started the farm.

They had around one-hundred-and-sixty-some acres. I lived with my grandparents. My mother died when I was about three years old. She had the flu in 1918. My dad took work on a farm over in Frankfort. I visited him very summer. He got married again when I was eight and then he took me.

"We raised hogs, chickens, ducks, geese. They'd always butcher in November, maybe one hog. After Christmas, they'd butcher two more. Maybe February they'd butcher another one. They had a smoke house. We made our lard when we butchered—rendered the fat, made cracklin' corn bread. My grandmother would grind the sausage, make patties out of it and fry it and put it in quart jars, pour grease over it, put it down in the cellar. She'd bring it up, slice it off and fry it. You don't get that kind of sausage anymore. They don't feed them like they used to.

"We made jelly and jam. Picked green beans and canned them. Grew sweet potatoes, navy beans. We sold eggs in Chillicothe. We had cows for milk, never butchered them, made butter, churned it. We had everything. They talk about the Depression. I don't remember too much about it. We had everything we needed."

Hannibal Hawk Williams was the grandfather of Clara Alfrieda Goodrich. His parents and grandparents were slaves on the plantation of Samuel Gist, a Virginia planter, banker and friend of George Washington. Gist lived in England, never came to the new colonies to see the backs of the slaves he stood on to climb the ladder of success. But he had a moral conversion; in his will, he left instructions to free all of the slaves upon his death, which occurred in 1815. Land agents were assigned to find property for the freedmen and in 1821, the ex-slaves were released in batches to be transported to Brown and Highland Counties in Ohio, to inhabit the rough and tumble farmland that had been left to them. They had no tools, no money, some deeds, no education, good luck—and look out for slave catchers out on the roads, hunting down freedman to fuel the slave markets booming in the South.

Hannibal was born on the Gist settlement in 1827.

Hannibal mustered into the Forty-fifth Regiment of the

USCT (U.S. Colored Troops) late in the Civil War, fought in the battle for Washington, marched in the inaugural parade after Abraham Lincoln's re-election, joined the Army of the Potomac, crossed the James River on March 27, 1864, fought valiantly in the final siege of Petersburg, and witnessed Robert E. Lee's surrender to Ulysses S. Grant at Appomattox Court House, Virginia. He told Alfrieda how poorly clothed they were, blood from bleeding feet showing up on tracks where they marched, seeing dead soldiers frozen to death. Hannibal was sent to Texas after the war and was mustered out, one of the lucky ones to survive battles and deadly diseases that took thirty-eight thousand soldiers in the USCT regiments.

Hannibal came back to Brown County, bought land, farmed, preached, made woven baskets, held political gatherings on the back of his wagon to discuss local and national politics. His older children taught him how to write his name in order to do business. He filed a lawsuit in Brown County for the right to vote, and won.

"Hannibal Hawk Williams was an activist," Alfrieda says. "People listened to him."

Clara Geneva, the eleventh of thirteen children born to Hannibal and Eliza Jane Page, with her daughter, Clara Alfrieda Goodrich.

In 1837 my great-great-grandparents, Elizabeth and Robert Edwards, packed their four children and all their possessions in a two-horse jersey wagon covered with a canvas top, left Bucks County, Pennsylvania, and traveled for three weeks across Pennsylvania to New Lexington in Highland County, a Quaker stronghold.

The Society of Friends held to the doctrine of the Inner Light. Everyone has within a test of truth upon which she can rely. The doctrine opposed the binding character of authority, held that war was incompatible with the Christian spirit, and that slavery must be eradicated.

January 22, 1864
Clear and cool. I cleaned the cellar. The girls churned.
Jesse tramped clover seed until noon, came in sick, high fever and cough.
Robert gone to Lexington.
No strangers here today.

Elizabeth is seated. Robert is leaning on the fence.

The couple bought a farm. Elizabeth bore four more children, and in 1852 Robert built the large home with bricks he made on the farm. The Edwards' home was an anchor in the community and a "safe house" on the Underground Railroad.

Joining a clandestine movement was not common practice among Quakers, even those who were abolitionists. Direct action protest was thought to be aggressive by orthodox Quakers, who sought to avoid conflict. But Elizabeth and Robert Edwards were Hicksites, the "un-programmed," progressive branch of Quakers who actively resisted state-sanctioned violence.

Although they were pacifists, their son, William, my great-grandfather, joined the Union army in 1861 and served four years in the killing fields as a medic.

"Because of sleeping out in a tent or in the field for so many years, his back bothered him; and he used to lie on the floor with his back to the fireplace, so the heat would ease his back pains," my mother writes.

In a letter dated *November 8, 1864, Natchez, Mississippi,* Will wrote to his sister Abigail in Ohio. Prisoners have been returned that day, and Abraham Lincoln was just elected.

"The boys have seen hard times. Some of our new recruits talk about having short rations, but I guess if they had to serve a turn in a Rebel prison, they would find out what short rations was… I don't know as it makes any difference who is elected, for I think the war will go on just the same. We have just so many men to kill anyhow before the thing can be settled, and I believe, if we have good luck, we will get through killing some time next summer. Perhaps you will call me wicked for talking so, but if you had been in this war as long as I, you would say kill very last one of them."

Will calls me over to the bookshelf where he sits, serious and intense. Look, I served and made it back home, and that's why you're here.

Will mustered out in Galveston, Texas, returned to Ohio and married Sadie, who birthed Grace who birthed Edith who birthed me.

But 620,000 soldiers did not come home from the killing fields. Civil War historians believe some 50,000 civilians died, most of these souls in the South.

Civil War Memorial, Hillsboro

War memorials glorify war, name the dead, call on the living to see the costs of war, as if that's what it takes to have a democracy.

Sadie   Grace and Edith

I open the hefty *Edwards Holy Bible* to Sadie's elegantly scripted record of births and deaths. William was twenty-six years old when he posed for the photograph in his Civil War uniform. He became a "heavy drinker," Mom writes; and Sadie "washed her boys' mouths out with lye soap" when they came home from Will's sawmill "cussing and swearing."

I randomly open to Matthew 6:39: *Ye have heard it said an eye for an eye and a tooth for a tooth, but I say unto you, resist not him that is evil.*

March 13
Clear and spring like, another sugar day.
I baked and got a letter from Will in Texas. All well.
The girls went to meeting.
No strangers here today.

143

OPINION

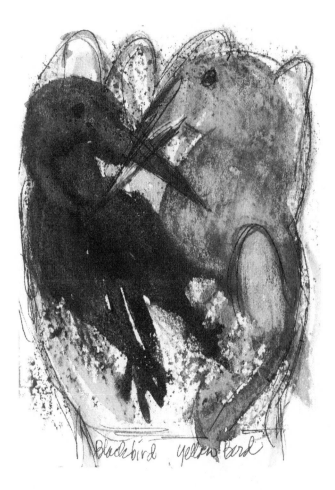

Writing is an act of faith, not a trick of grammar.
E.B. White

IT WAS RULED

Merle Hudson, Gertrude Clemons Hudson,
Joyce Clemons Kittrell, 2006

Joyce Clemmons Kittrell: "They had to have a Plaintiff. A mother with a child. Mom said, 'We'll use Joyce.' Other parents were afraid. They threatened to take kids from their moms, intimidating the moms. I was kind of shy. If I saw cameras, I would move to the back. Mom would protect me. Reporters came to our house and took pictures. I went to the trial here in Hillsboro and once in Cincinnati.

"Mom taught me how to handle it, how to carry myself, how to put myself in a position that is strong. It was a lot to think about as a child. Try to look at people, who they are, relate to them. Listen and then you'll know how to talk to them. She was firm. She wanted us to know what we were doing and how we were doing it. I always wanted to march."

Gertrude: "The judge told me to stand up and raise my right hand. I stood up and raised my right hand and he looked at Motley and he looked at me and told me to take my hand down and sit down. It was completed. It was ruled. They had to let them go to school."

On January 5, 1956, Judge Potter Stewart wrote the majority opinion of the Court of Appeals in *Clemons v. Board of Education of Hillsboro, Ohio*:

"*The Hillsboro Board of Education created the gerrymandered school districts after the Supreme Court had announced its first opinion in the segregation cases. The board's action was, therefore... in knowing violation of the Constitution of the United States... The avoidance alone of somewhat overcrowded classrooms cannot justify segregation of school children solely because of the color of their skins.*"

A young black female attorney winning a case in a higher court presided over by a white female judge, ruling in favor of a group of uppity colored mothers?

District Court Judge John Druffel wouldn't budge.

James Hapner: "John Druffel influenced us to take our case to the Supreme Court. John Druffel Jr. was the man who took it to the Supreme Court for us. They denied *certiorari* (a full review), upholding the Sixth Circuit decision, and we were ordered to admit the children of the plaintiffs. They hadn't been in school at this stage for almost two years."

Judge Druffel refused to proceed until all the paperwork found its way from the high courts to his cherry desk in Cincinnati and then, to Superintendent Upp's solid oak desk in Hillsboro, which is when *Time Magazine* caught up with the story:

"... But the Hillsboro board was not through yet. At first it stalled until it formally received Judge Druffel's order. Then it hit upon the idea of ordering placement tests for the Negroes who had been tutored at home. To convince everyone of its objectivity, it invited the State Department of Education to supervise the testing, only to find that the department had no such tests on hand and would have to get them from Chicago. At week's end the test duly arrived. The last bastion of segregation in Ohio had finally fallen."[9]

Segregation fallen?

Gertrude: "What seemed so horrible to me was when the kids had to take a test. That's the part that really hurt me. The kids had to go back a grade. They let on like every one of them failed the test."

Higher Than Expected

When the tests came back from the state department, Mary Hackney, the Quaker teacher who helped teach in the Kitchen Schools, was not given the results. She went to the Superintendent's office. "And so I said, 'I don't understand this. Where are my tests?'

"'Well,' he says, 'I don't know what Mr. Upp did with that bunch.' And I got to lookin. There was a thing on top of the desk with papers filed in it and down under there was... you know, I was a teacher, I knew what they looked like. If he'd have been quick enough to just put that thing down under the desk, I'd have never known. And finally I said to him, I said, 'You say you don't have the tests?'

"'No, I don't know what Mr. Upp did with them.'

"And I said, 'They look like they're right there under those papers in that holder. Will you look and see? Maybe Mr. Upp put them in there in piles and said, don't give these out because they'll claim that those kids are doing all right.'

"He said, 'Well now, Mrs. Hackney, you can't expect one day a week will keep them up with public school work where the teachers have them every day.'

"I said, 'I had them under Miss Kilgore when I wasn't there and she was the best you'll ever have in any public school.

"'Well,' he says, 'I don't know. She isn't a teacher, Miss Kilgore.'

"I said, 'Oh, but she is. She may not have her degree, but she one of the best I've ever had. And you'd be lucky to have her in your school. Will you look and see if those are the tests? Maybe he forgot to lay them out.'

"And he looked and I said, 'Oh, here they are.'

"Well I was shocked; they were so high! Higher than I expected."

MAPS

Teresa Williams: "A lot of times, people didn't understand this. Our books were not even up to standard. If we were reading geography and they were talking about Africa, they'd let the black kids read. Anything else, they wouldn't call on blacks to read. Bob Stanforth came over to my house after he saw the play and said, 'Teresa, I didn't know that stuff was going on.' I was in the fifth grade with him. We were friends. The ones who were nasty and prejudiced had to hear it at home. They called me Sixteen Tons, Snowflakes, Cream Puff. Willard Parr Jr.—I tried to shove him out of the window on the second floor. We took a lot. Our dad told us, 'Don't come home crying because if you do, I'm going to give you a whipping.'

"There were some good teachers out there, ones that really cared about the kids. Miss Fels. Mr. McElwee. Harold Spargur. He broke it down. If you failed, it was your fault. He took time."

Joyce Clemons Kittrell: "They made us take the fifth grade over when we got into school. When we went into fifth grade, all of a sudden, they come with this rule. We're going to have a lower class of kids who can't make this grade and an upper class of kids who can make this grade. And blacks aren't going to make it. But it didn't always work out that way. The parents were pushing us hard. Do the best you can. The majority of us got in that upper class. We worked hard. We studied hard.

"We had math, reading, English. I remember them talking about science and geography. Subjects we'd never heard of. Maps. We never had maps. How do you read a map? We'd never seen a map before. So when the teacher pulled these big maps down, this was new to us."

FRIENDSHIP

On one of those days that feels brand new, when the cold and barren Midwest winter turns the corner to spring, and redbuds burst into magenta, and daffodils break through the brown earth announcing *yellow,* Doris Cumberland finally walks through the doors of Webster Elementary, into Mrs. Mallory's classroom, and sits in my row behind Hughie Bowline.

Doris Cumberland Woods: "I was scared, nervous. It seemed like everyone was staring. The first few days my mother went with me to school. Mrs. Mallory eased my fear. Out on the playground, she would say things to me. She would talk to me about things that were going on, about my feelings, adjusting to being in the classroom, the kids that were there. She really wanted me to adjust. The learning was different. It was all different. Everything was different. I didn't really know anything about the white culture.

"Then after a while certain kids—kind of adjusted to me being there because—Tamara Rogers—maybe it was Connie—somebody was having a birthday party and just about everybody in the class was invited to it, and I got an invitation to go. My mother wouldn't let me go. She was scared to let me go."

"I can vaguely remember the fire, a lot of confusion going on, back and forth. When it got dark, they would ride through the black neighborhood and burn crosses, throw bottles. I remember that."

Doris and I can't remember anyone explaining much of anything. Our anxieties and questions disappeared into the social ethers above town, and Hillsboro went back to its segregated habits. The fallout from the *Brown* decision landed on the desks of the teachers and in the hearts of kids who had to connect the dots between those big legal concepts.

Doris lives in Cincinnati, works graveyard shift as a nurse's aid in a big hospital, goes in at eleven p.m., works all night, gets home at seven, sleeps until two, gets up to fix her husband supper, then back to work.

I try to see the skinny, shy Doris who has held a featured place in my memory for so long, but another Doris sits on her sectional couch, a full-grown woman, gracious and warm. We talk about how we both loved Mrs. Mallory, who was reading the white kids *Charlotte's Web* while the black kids were outside the window, marching with their moms.

"If you were Charlotte," I ask Doris, "what word would you choose to weave into the web—to save the world?"

She takes her time to think about it, and while she does, I feel in her gentle attitude, some kind of permission to relax and take in this moment that began mysteriously in our childhood, connecting us to now.

"*Friendship*," Doris says, "for everybody just to try friendship. That's hard to do."

Doris Cumberland Woods, 2003

Belong

Every day I awaken torn between the desire
to save the world and the inclination to savor it.
E.B. White

PART III

THE BACKSTORY

Bell's Opera House, Hillsboro

The film grows as you are making it,
like a relationship with a person.
Federico Fellini

Characters in order of appearance

Voiced text from oral interviews, conversations, documents, cited sources

Secret Room
Eleanor Curtis Cumberland
Orloff Miller Jr.
Doug and Diana McKay
Janet Larkin
Elizabeth Conard Edwards

Inside Job
Lewis Goins
Clara Alfrieda Goodrich
Reverend Fred Shuttlesworth
Dr. Martin Luther King, Jr.
John Lewis, U.S. House of Representatives
Sally Roush Rogers
Imogene Curtis
Annie Popkin
Fannie Lou Hamer
Malcolm X
David Ornette Cherry
Shirley Wimmer
Garry Boone
Rosemary Kinyanjui

If It Ain't Got That Swing
Philip Partridge
Tom Partridge
Elizabeth Partridge
Beth Partridge

The Shadow Play
Risa Boone
Joe Partridge
Dr. Manning Marable
Susan Williams
Patrice Lumumba
Che Guevara
Dag Hammarskjöld
Ossie Davis
Alex Haley
Edward Snowden
Chris Metro

Eye of the Law
George Fox
William Penn
Clara Alfrieda Goodrich
Judge Nathaniel Jones
Judge Constance Baker Motley
Justice John Marshall Harlan
Senator Frank Church
Michael Kean
Charles Glatt
David Ornette Cherry
Nicholas Katzenbach
Jack Quincy Davis
Saxophone Player

Beloved Kaleidoscope Community
John Bryant
Pam Limes
Rory Ryan
Drew Hastings

Betty Bishop
Tim Koehl
Joyce Clemons Kittrell
Virginia Harewood
Carolyn Goins
Teresa Williams
Elsie Steward Young
Lewis Goins
Tom Partridge
Edith Rhoten Banyas
John W. Banyas
Elizabeth Conard Edwards

Ohio River

White Oak Creek

Edwards Farm

Secret Room
Ohio, 2003

The first day I meet Eleanor, at Mrs. Goodrich's home with Elsie, having pie and starting the project by turning on the tape recorder, Eleanor describes her relationship to the forces that wanted to erase her from history.

Eleanor: "There's no black history taught in Hillsboro High School. The children today don't have anybody to relate to other than the basketball players, the rap artists, the entertainers. The drug dealer down the street gets more respect than me. I think they should be taught about the people who discovered things, made an impact. Without black history, kids lose their identity.

"For twenty-four years I did not have an identity at Highland District Hospital. I was that 'little colored girl.' I'm Eleanor Curtis Cumberland, daughter of Imogene and Orville Curtis. I have a husband, James, four children. I have a life. At my retirement party, I'm sure somebody will say, 'You know, that little colored girl is having a retirement party.' That's the truth!"

Eleanor describes tending to a patient who spat on her. The violence is unthinkable.

"Why would a patient spit on you?"

"You have to understand slavery, Susan," she says. "We are possessions to them. They are possessed."

I am standing in front of an exhibit at the National Underground Railroad Freedom Center in Cincinnati—oceans of blue water held in a tank, marbles at the bottom of the ocean, the routes of the global slave trade from Africa to the Americas etched into the glass. The marbles represent the thousands of people who were thrown overboard into the sea alive to alleviate crowded conditions, who suffocated to death in compartments eighteen inches deep, side by side, chained down, who died from grief and disease during the Middle Passage.

This is how the American Empire was built. The men who wrote the Constitution built their wealth this way, then wrote a document about freedom. This was the original coup, the original state of possession, passing as democracy.

Orloff Miller, Jr., archivist and historian at the Freedom Center, graciously agrees to drive out to the Edwards farm on Underground Road in Highland County to examine the evidence of the backstory of my kin. His father was one of the three clergymen beaten outside a café in Selma when they went south to answer Dr. King's call. One of the trio, James Reeb, died from the injuries.

The current owners of the farm, Doug and Diana McKay, show us through the "safe house," from the stone foundation and thick floor joists and beams to the second floor, where Elizabeth sat at her writing desk to reflect on the day, noting the rhythms and work of farm life, the movement of Strangers. Orloff fills in the scene.

Strangers moved at night from farm to farm, pursued by slavecatchers backed by federal law, who were hunting down fugitives, kidnapping free blacks, transporting the human "property" back to the masters in the South, collecting their bounty.

Strangers escaped during winter holidays, when the masters partied, across the Ohio River at Ripley, moved up creeks to throw the bloodhounds off. "Conductors" sent them up through Brown County into Highland County. The network was local and hidden from sheriffs and potential traitors. The consequences were grave—prison, confiscation of the farm, and for *Strangers*, forced marches, slave markets, and worse.

The McKays have invited an elderly gentleman who lived on the farm in the 1930s to join us. He remembers shimmying down the cistern where there was a small door large enough to crawl into. Inside was a nine-foot square room adjoining the well, about seven feet high, with an arched ceiling and two flat stones that may have been seats. When he found the secret room, he says, it was painted white and perfectly clean.

The cistern is now covered by a two-car garage off the porch. A road crew found the secret room, according to a newspaper article in 1947.

Orloff is down on his hands and knees on the porch, trying to locate the memory.

We drive to Hillsboro to the home of Janet Larkin, Catherine Ingersoll's daughter, who has inherited Elizabeth's diary. Orloff examines the little book. Yes, he affirms.

Elizabeth Edwards and her family had quietly joined the scattered grassroots resistance movement that grew into a vast network of free blacks, preaching women, pastors, newspapers, wealthy patrons, progressive politicians, former slaves on the abolitionist lecture circuits, "station masters," "conductors," and Friends, who outsmarted slave catchers and U.S. marshals, to become what Henry David Thoreau called *"a counter-friction to the machine,"* the first human rights movement in the country's history to challenge the "economic system."

JANUARY.

1.

1864

I arose this morning 1 minutes of 5 found it very cold thermometer, 16 degrees below Zero blowing, strong no strangers here but Haidee, the girls sewing at Marias dress men potting around. too cold to work

2.

INSIDE JOB

I believe that is the happy cynicism of a creative mind, to wit, believing that you came into this world for the unique goal of narrating it to others.

Federico Fellini

LIGHTNING BUGS IN A JAR

There we are on our last day in Mrs. Mallory's class, cleaning out our grubby little desks, gathering our stubby crayons, and heading into the summer of 1956.

Mom has a two-tone red and white convertible. She releases the latches above the visors, pushes a button, and the top of the car lifts off, lurches forward, then gracefully bends backwards and folds itself up behind the back seat. We stretch a leather cover over the contraption, snap it down, and perch on top like parade queens.

We prowl the neighborhood bragging about everything we know, smell and snoop, compare calf muscles, count each minute of the clock to make sure there are sixty like they say. There are.

On hot nights, we run around outside in shorty pajamas and catch lightning bugs, snatch them as they light up in the grass and put them in mason jars. We poke holes in the lids with ice picks so the lightning bugs can breathe, and carry our little glass lanterns around in the dark corners of our territory.

The fields around our houses sparkle with thousands of lightning bugs.

Magic is all around no matter what side of town you come from.

Chocolate Drop

Then back to the fourth grade. Mr. West is the complete opposite of Mrs. Mallory. He wears a brown suit, brown tie, brown shoes and is strictly no-nonsense. We have to stand in front of the class and recite the Gettysburg Address and Henry Wadsworth Longfellow.

Under the spreading chestnut tree the village smithie stands.
The smith a mighty man is he with large and sinewy hands.
And the muscles of his brawny arms are as strong as iron bands.

I stand in line to go down the slide and stare at one of the new colored kids, Lewis, who leaps up the ladder, swings from the handles at the top of the slide, and pops off at the bottom like an acrobat. Where did he come from?

Lewis Goins: "Adams Street. We lived on a dead end. We had about thirty or forty acres back there. My granddad was a brick mason. He was one of the only ones in Ohio who could hand-cut stone. My grandparents raised me. My mom worked at Wright Pat (Wright Patterson Air Force Base near Dayton). I came along and she was living with Grandma and Grandpa. I'm the oldest of twelve. Lewis, Lawrence, Lee, Lloyd, Leonard, Leslie, Lonny, Libby, Lynne, Lisa, Lemoin, and Lorraine."

I find Lewis at the Fiftieth reunion of Lincoln School, the beloved cultural hub of the African American community in Hillsboro from the time it was built in 1869, during Reconstruction, until the school board closed the doors in 1956, fourscore and seven years later. The testimony is alive with pride for the school, alumni accomplishments, gratitude to the teachers, and soul food prepared and served by the women in the community, who seem like love glue.

"What happened to Lincoln?" I ask Lewis.

"They sold it and one of the funeral directors stored caskets in it for a while, then they tore it down." Lewis says.

Caskets?

Lewis is wearing a Vietnam Vet's cap and is forthcoming and friendly, like we're still on the same kickball team. Yes, I can interview him. Lewis and Carolyn Goins live across the street from where Lincoln School used to stand, nestled in the trees, where Philip Partridge lit the match that sparked the story.

"We had to walk by the Washington School to go to Lincoln. But then going back home, kids would start calling us names. About every day. Yep. We had a bad time getting back across town. Fights. Oh yeah.

"What always fascinated me—our parents took care of those peoples' kids, was house cleaners, cooks, but we couldn't go to school together..

"I went to Miss Boots, a fantastic lady." Miss Boots was Lewis' Kitchen School teacher during the two-year protest.

"She always wore boots. She used to drive Rooney's Cab, worked for Doris Rooney, up near the Fire Department. She was kind."

Lewis left the kindness of Miss Boots and entered the new culture. "When we finally got into Webster, they put us back a year. Mr. West was alright. He lived on East Main Street, a pretty good old guy.

"The only trouble we had was the poor white kids. One day I went in the bathroom and Terry Cole called me a chocolate drop. And so I grabbed him and stuck his head in the toilet. From that day on I never had no trouble with Terry Cole. That was about the extent of it.

"My granddad died when I was fourteen and we had a hard time. We were living off a little social security check— me and my grandmother and Aunt Patty and my sister, that's all we lived off of. I had to quit school at sixteen and go to work. I started washing cars up at Kenny's Auto Laundry. We washed cars for your dad. Then I left there and went to McGee's, washing dishes for Denver Magee. I worked eight hours there. Then I went out the back door and worked six hours a day at the Sundry Store stocking shelves. I was supporting the family. That's what kept us going. Then I got on at Rotary Forms Press. They make business forms. I remember your Dad and Charlie Limes real well."

Lewis had placed his medals on the coffee table. "Do people in Hillsboro know you are a decorated Vet, Lewis?"

"No," he said. "No one knows that."

THE MAN UPSTAIRS

Lewis Goins: "August of '67 I got my draft letter from Lyndon Baines Johnson. I was in the Tet of '68 and the Tet of '69. Tet is the Vietnamese Lunar New Year. Our first big battle was on a rubber plantation. I spent eleven months and twenty-six days in Vietnam with the One Hundred and First Airborne Division. We lived in the jungle, out in the boonies anywhere from sixty to ninety days at a time. We were always the first ones in and last ones out. I was always on the first chopper in. All over Vietnam... I've been all over.

"Down south it was rice paddies. When you go north, you get into the mountains and jungles. You wore stuff till it rotted off—shoes would rot on you. Underwear rotted away.

"A hundred to a hundred-and-fifty pounds on your back. I carried a little Bible with a plastic cover. I had to carry an M16. It wouldn't fire in the rain. Russians supplied the Viet Cong with AK47s, the best weapon.

"The platoon leader lays his map out on the trail, which he's never done. That was a cardinal sin. When you brought out a map and compass, they knew you were a leader. All of sudden I heard a pop. AK47s made a pop. And he hollered for me and when I got to him, he was dead.

"RPG—a nasty weapon, a very nasty weapon. When a guy gets hit with one of them, it would blow him apart. We had to pick up body parts. A guy's arm laying here, a leg laying there and you know, match it up with the guys there. For politicians, it was a conflict. People got slaughtered over there. People got killed every day. Every day. It was bad, bad.

"They talk about people of color can't be leaders because they weren't smart enough. The white people had their loopholes. People who couldn't go to college, you signed up for the draft. People of color—all of us were in leadership positions. I was the Platoon Sergeant. I had forty-two men that I had to watch out for. I never lost a man.

"We were sent to relieve the 4th infantry division. They were wiped out. There were only four guys left. We had to get the U.S. bodies off the hill. Then we had to bury all the NVA (Viet Cong). We spent two weeks doing that. That's when we got the letter that MLK was assassinated.

"For some reason or another The Man Upstairs brought me home. We had no help when we came home. No programs. No counseling. The nightmares, problems, you had to deal on your own. Children were coming up deformed.

"I went back to my job at Rotary Forms. My insurance wouldn't cover psychiatry. I quit taking my Lexipro. My feet and hands went numb. I couldn't run a forklift and be in la la land. Been my own doctor for all these years, me and her (Carolyn). She's put up with a lot of junk over the years. All the wives have. At the reunion, the wives have their little powwows.

"We went to the reunion in '03. That's when I finally figured it out. PTSD. We all had the same problems—depression, flashback, moodiness, don't want to be around people, anxiety attacks, hot flashes. I haven't slept since '68. My day starts at one a.m. You got attacked either right at dark or daybreak. In that picture (veterans' reunion picture), probably seventy-five percent of them have some type of cancer. Kidneys. Bone cancer. We all have the same opinion. The government lied to us… it was all politics. We lost fifty-eight thousand men and women (another fifty-eight thousand to suicides). I don't like the system and I don't like the government. They sprayed Agent Orange on us. Up North they sprayed all the time. Now it's oil. They're over there fighting for oil."

Lewis received a Bronze Star, Army Commendation

Medal, Combat Infantryman Badge, Air Medal, and Vietnam Service Medal for his *outstanding meritorious service in ground operations,* for his *untiring efforts and professional ability,* for his *initiative, zeal, sound judgment, devotion to duty,* and for his ability to *grasp the implications of new problems with which he was faced as a result of the ever-changing situations.*

"I do a little praying in the morning when I get up, then move on. I'll make the best of it until The Man Upstairs calls me home."

Who is Silent

Fifth grade is the year of spit wads. We are horrible to Miss Hedges, fresh out of college. One day she cries in class, and I feel bad for her, but laugh hysterically when Hughie Ballein fakes a fart.

In sixth grade, Mrs. Barre opens up our world through letters to pen pals in Germany. My pen pal, Helga, lives in Stuttgart and sends me a pink hankie with a yellow baby chick in the corner, for Christmas. Helga's stationary is thin and lacy, and her handwriting is slanted to the left and stylish. I can't imagine how she can come from the same country as Hitler, not that I remember ever discussing Hitler at school or anywhere. How did I find out?

The heavy, musty *Life's Picture History of World War II* was my childhood history book, fascinating as a kid. What did it say about Hitler? There is one small picture of Hitler in the book. He is staring at the ruins of Germany. Shortly after the photo was taken, the caption reads "… he put a bullet through his head and was carried out of his bunker, along with his dead mistress, both of them doused with gasoline, and set on fire by the SS. The remains were never found." There are no pictures of the death camps in the book, no reference to the Holocaust, and the book ends with a two-page color spread of the mushroom cloud in all its glory—the photos of the quarter of a million women and children and old people who were incinerated or died from radioactive poisoning were suppressed until recently.

The last page is a black and white portrait of a gritty American soldier, cigarette dangling from his mouth, an ordinary man, a warrior, taken by the gutsy photojournalist, W. Eugene Smith, who later quit *Life*. He didn't want the corporation controlling his content.

Charlie Limes was one of the soldiers in those D-day pictures. He smoked two packs a day and died too young. The book is a media production, the theatre of war, the death cult in all its glory. I give the book to Goodwill. A delicate hankie, a memory of a distant friendship, stays tucked in the corner of my underwear drawer.

In Ohio History, we learn about the Erie Canal, but there is not a peep about the two-year protest staged by the marching mothers of Hillsboro that led to their victory in the first desegregation battle north of the Mason Dixon Line after *Brown*. In Current Events, we look at a map of Indochina and hear about the Domino Theory, but the testy Miss Fels never pulls down the map of America and directs her pointer at Birmingham, Alabama. I never hear the name *Constance Baker Motley*, who has gone head to head in the Sixth Circuit Court of Appeals with James Hapner, my Latin teacher's son. Mrs. Hapner always looks like she forgot to brush her hair, glasses propped precariously on her nose, an excellent Latin teacher.

Qui tacet consentire. Who is silent gives consent.

New Social Rules

The summer between my freshman and sophomore years of high school, my parents pack us up, and off we go to a bigger life, thirty-eight miles due east, in Chillicothe, a paper mill town that smells like my dad's farts after Grandma Bufton's cabbage rolls. Dad buys a Pontiac-Cadillac dealership—even though we've always been a Buick family. I wave goodbye to Pam and Danville Pike. Life is never the same after that. No one talks about feelings.

New social rules. No cigarettes if you're a cheerleader, not that I smoke. Must wear Weegins. Must act cool. I quit the band, quit going to church, quit singing in the choir, quit diving, quit going out with my so-called boyfriend, who drops me off and then goes down the street to his Catholic girlfriend's house, where they get it on.

Mom finds a piano teacher for me, a black musician named Sonny Harris, who comes over to the house and teaches me how to play "Misty"—how to go inside the time and sound of the notes to find the feeling of the music, to get with the dream of it. I love playing "Misty," but quit taking lessons. I don't know why. I just quit.

Country and western music from the Chicken Inn floats across the highway, up the hill to the front porch where I swing back and forth, back and forth, back and forth, wondering why I feel so lost.

While I battle the blues in Ohio, black teens in Birmingham, Alabama battle Bull Conner. School children of all ages take to the streets to protest segregation for three days—the Children's Crusade. The Superintendent of Public Safety, Eugene "Bull" Conner, releases attack dogs, blasts kids into walls and down the streets with power hoses strong enough to rip bark off a tree. Americans watch it on TV, shocked at the violence, angry at blacks for stirring up trouble, angry at Kennedy for letting it happen.

Constance Baker Motley goes down to Birmingham to engineer the reinstatement of the eleven hundred children who had been expelled from schools during the protest. She successfully defends Martin Luther King Jr. in Georgia and Ralph Abernathy and Fred Shuttlesworth in Alabama.

"Call up Reverend Shuttlesworth," the wise and scholarly Mrs. Clara Alrieda Goodrich advises. "He lives in Cincinnati now. He was pastor at the Zion Baptist Church. He had surgery recently, but he might see you." She mails a beautiful note in her elegant handwriting and encloses a white hankie with lace trim and a piece of paper with the name, address, and phone number of the Reverend Fred Shuttlesworth— the man who stood up to Bull Conner in Birmingham Alabama—the man who faced down fear.

"Lovingly, Alfrieda."

You Can't Outdo Mr. God
June 2006, Cincinnati, Ohio

A strikingly handsome man wearing a royal blue shirt, the civil rights warrior opens the door of his modest house. He invites me in. "I hope you're not going to make Hillsboro become just as *bad* as Birmingham Alabama. I would suspect many places that were thought to be exceedingly nice might be found to be wanting in that respect." He smiles.

I am in the presence of an extraordinary person and everything is normal—the kitchen, the couch, the coffee table, the coffee. I smile back. Then he takes me to Birmingham.

Fred Shuttlesworth: "Birmingham was as low as you could get outside of Johannesburg, South Africa. At that time there were fourteen lawsuits against me. The city was suing me, and I was suing the city. The NAACP Legal Defense Fund took the cases over. They sent Norman Attica, Thurgood, and Constance Motley. She was genuine. She was the first black woman federal judge. Beautiful woman, kind of motherly.

"I was in jail about thirty-some times. When I was arrested, I was put in with drunks. I put in a petition to integrate the jail. Sure. I wasn't afraid. It became almost an obsession to me... I always kept something going. On Christmas eve night, 1956, the Klan moved.

"A bomb went off in my house next to the church. The roof came down. The floor was blown out from under the bed. My bed was right up against the wall. The dynamite destroyed that wall. The front wall went almost into the street. And yet there I was among it.

"1956—I'm challenging everything—railroad stations, buses. When the supreme court outlawed segregation on the buses in Montgomery, I asked the city officials—Bull Conner, Damon Morgan, Wagner, the three commissioners—to rescind and relax the law in light of the Supreme Court decision and whether you like it or not, we're going to ride buses anyway.

"They castrated a black man to send me word.

"The Klan beat me up in front of Philips High School in 1957 when I intended to enroll my kids. I was almost killed in front of the school. I think the abuse I took at Birmingham laid the basis. The students took it up—interstate buses, freedom rides, sit ins.

"So we got the laws turned around. You must remember the federal government—local city officials like Bull Conner—they weren't going to enforce anything. They wouldn't protect us. So we were beaten and attacked. The courts still don't honor mass integration. It takes years to work that out.

"The Democratic party has been very inept. The country has fascist tendencies and uses fascist methods. Pre-emptive situations. We want to get a deep footing into the oil fields where we are in control. Right-wing ideas have taken over this country and have dominated the three agencies of the federal government.

"There is a pride in America. America calls itself a godly nation. We're not acting godly. We never have, not since slavery. Evil gets more evil as it runs rampant. Is the land healed? Look at what happened in New Orleans. They haven't cleaned it up yet. And it will get worse. Now you can mass produce what you want to, but it's bleeding us of everything that's precious and dear in our lives. Everything is power and position.

"You can't outdo Mr. God. He sits upon the circle of the earth. In *Isaiah,* it tells how He regards people as grasshoppers. We think we're a superpower. He calls us grasshoppers. You can't bomb people's houses and make them love you.

"Sharing, lifting, why can't we do that with the Muslim countries? Only by spirituality can we all come together."

He walks me to the door. Fred Shuttlesworth kisses me on the lips, a blessing, a warrior's blessing.

Inside Job

In the summer of '63, I get my first job at Woolworth's in the clothing department selling cotton undies and square cotton slacks and square cotton blouses. I learn to make change at the cash register and deposit my earnings into a savings account in order to earn interest.

Over in Hillsboro, the leader of the marching mothers, Imogene Curtis, boards a bus heading to Washington, D.C. Along with a quarter million other people, she answers the call to come to the capitol and join the largest human rights demonstration in the history of the nation.

"The arc of the moral universe is long, but it bends toward justice." Dr. King's words are etched into time, up there in the cosmos. John Lewis is twenty-one years old. He steps up to the podium and looks out at the sea of faces that stretch down the Mall to the Lincoln Memorial. Imogene Curtis is out there listening. "We must get with the revolution," he says.

A few days later, on September 15, 1963, a bomb goes off in the Sixteenth Street Baptist Church in Birmingham, the Klan's response to the March on Washington. Four little girls—Denise McNair, Cynthia Wesley, Carole Robertson, and Addie Mae Collins, in a Sunday School class, in their church outfits, humming a hymn, dabbling with a pencil, straightening a sock, staring at the light dancing across a wall—are blown to bits.

This never comes up at school. None of it.

Our World History teacher, Mr. Ladd, is tired of Babylon and tired of us but not tired of the bottle tucked away in his desk drawer. He spends half the period writing questions on the chalkboard for us to answer, and we spend the other half of the period writing the questions in our notebooks. History is way off in the distance.

Until it comes over the loud speaker in typing class.

President Kennedy has been shot. We are sent home from school. I watch my dad crying in the front of the TV. The horse-drawn hearse marches through the streets of the nation's capital—clip clop, clip clop—the death dirge, the end of Camelot.

I watch Jack Ruby shoot Lee Harvey Oswald on TV, then go to the school dance. I don't believe Ruby died of a "heart attack" in prison. I grew up on *Nancy Drew* and *Perry Mason*. I can spot the criminals. LBJ didn't seem sincere on that airplane with Jackie, getting sworn in, blood from President Kennedy's blasted head still on Jackie's pink suit. I am only fifteen, but it is clear to me that the whole thing was an inside job.

THE DOT GROWS BIGGER

In Mr. Baker's economics class, I learn about interest rates and bull markets. Mr. Baker puts his pen in his white shirt pocket while he lectures. The pen starts to leak and bleed through Mr. Baker's cotton shirt, a small black dot. My eyes are glued to his pocket. The dot grows bigger and starts slowly spreading out, and he doesn't know it.

I get an A for my report in American History on the postal service, inspired by Grandpa Rhoten, who was the postmaster of Mowrystown, Ohio before he died in 1955.

But over in Hillsboro, American History is being created. My Hillsboro buddy Sally Roush Rogers recalls the incident: "You were gone. We had an American history teacher—Luther Warren—who was a PhD in history. He was one of the most eccentric teachers you could have. Our class invited Mrs. Curtis in to talk about the March on Washington (Imogene Curtis). Mrs. Curtis talked about how important the march was, how things were going to have to change. I don't remember much about it, except that it set off a firestorm. The phones started ringing off the superintendent's desk. People did not want those black troublemakers coming in and talking to the kids at the school. They wanted that man out of there because he was perverting the children. Dr. Warren was a pacifist and a Quaker, so he was very active on social issues. His contract was not renewed. At the end of the year, he was gone. Harry Bennett was the Superintendent at that time. When we heard he was going to be fired, we all protested. Remember those cool ties? Well, Dr. Warren still wore those old ties from the '40s. So all of us got our dads to lend us old ties and we declared Luther Warren day. We all thought Dr. Warren was cool."

UNARMED TRUTH

In the hot, sticky summer of 1964, I am working for my dad in the office at Banyas Pontiac-Cadillac, typing up car titles and finance contracts and counting money by day, and dancing to the Temptations out at Ater's Lake with my new boyfriend, Steve, by night.

Mississippi Freedom Summer breezes right by me.

My sister, Martha, is going to college at Miami University in Oxford, Ohio, but I don't have a clue that students are pouring into Oxford that summer to be trained in non-violent, direct action tactics, in order to go door to door to register black voters, be support staff, and teach in the "freedom schools." The Mississippi Summer Project of 1964, designed to put the spotlight on the growing black power movement emerging from Mississippi, by inviting white allies to participate in the revolution-- a thousand volunteers answered the call—this courageous and brilliant orchestration of democratic process never appeared on my radar screen. I don't remember any dinner conversation about how the leaders of this movement appealed to Attorney General Robert Kennedy and President Johnson for federal protection, but were refused.

My friend, Annie Popkin, was one of those students, a radical from the East Coast, who went to Oxford that summer. Her parents had cocktail parties to raise money for supplies, books, clothes to send down to Mississippi.[10]

The sweet corn is at its best two weeks before the 1964 Democratic convention opens in Atlantic City. They have just found the bullet-riddled, beaten bodies of three of the students—Mickey Schwerner, Andrew Goodman, and James Chaney—buried near a dam in Philadelphia, Mississippi.[11] Rita Schwerner makes the announcement in Oxford.

Annie calls her parents. Her group is about to leave for the South. Her parents are terrified, but tell her on the phone that it's her decision. She boards the bus.

"They were trying to send us a message," Annie says. "There were still five hundred students in Oxford, and they wanted to scare us away from going South. Most went. We stayed with families. I shared a bed with another civil rights worker. The parents left to pick cotton early in the morning, would sleep in the afternoon. We had the bed in-between. I'd never seen a two-inch cockroach. I registered voters, went through the neighborhoods with my partner, a young black woman from Vicksburg, knocking on doors. People were suspicious, but then would invite us in. They always had photographs of MLK, Jesus, and John Kennedy.

"I loved the church and wrote to a friend about being so swept into the spiritual energy that I took communion. She told my mom, 'Something's wrong with Annie. She took communion.' My mom said, 'Oh no, she's just taken up with the excitement and all.' My mom was progressive, thank goodness.

"We were warned not to go into the white neighborhoods. I did once for some reason, and someone tried to run me down with a car, and I didn't know where to go for help. I couldn't think about the terror or I couldn't have done what I needed to do. We had strength in numbers."

Annie writes to her friend: "Ran, this is something really big—yes, a revolution—a new way of Living and Being…a clear path—this is where the great Change will come. There is hope here that isn't in the North.'"

The Democratic convention is on TV in all of its pageantry. But the Democratic Party refuses to seat the black delegation from Mississippi, the Freedom Democrats led by Fanny Lou Hamer, one of the organizers of Mississippi Freedom Summer. She puts it on the line:

"If the Mississippi Freedom Democratic Party is not seated now, I question America. Is this America, the land of the free and the home of the brave where we have to sleep with our telephones off the hooks because our lives be threatened daily because we want to live as decent human beings in America?"

Lyndon Johnson wins the nomination and a landslide victory, but Fannie Lou Hamer has the last word. "No one is free until everyone is free."

Annie: "I didn't talk about this for twenty years. When I got back, the SDS students called me a liberal do-gooder and the Black Power students called me whitey. I had felt the injustice when I was five years old, and mom drove into a different neighborhood and I saw poverty for the first time and it changed me. Race and gender and class have been defining issues in my work and in my life."[12]

Over in Oslo, Dr. Martin Luther King, Jr. is awarded the Nobel Peace Prize. "Christ gave us the goals and Mahatma Gandhi the tactics," he says in his acceptance speech. "I refuse to accept the cynical notion that nation after nation must spiral down a militaristic stairway into the hell of thermonuclear destruction. I believe that unarmed truth and unconditional love will have the final word in reality."

Johnson escalates the Vietnam War through a scorched earth policy and the use of napalm on other human beings *and* signs into passage the Civil Rights Act of 1964 and the Voting Rights Act of 1965. Blacks can finally vote and hold public office *and* are sent to Vietnam in disproportionate numbers to save the world from Communism and die and kill other people for the freedom and opportunity they are denied in Georgia and Detroit and Hillsboro.

Trigonometry

I am a Mathlete, and the proof is in the Chillicothe High School Cavaliers Yearbook, which is good since I have zero memory of trigonometry my senior year. Something about how you angle things. Angles. Spatial dynamics. Pattern recognition.

Malcolm X is connecting the dots between the freedom movements in America and the anti-colonial movements in Africa. Look at the power system. Think. Study history. Seek your truth. "I realized racism isn't just a black and white problem. It's brought bloodbaths to about every nation on earth at one time or another," he says in an interview with photographer and filmmaker Gordon Parks.

But Malcolm X is a non-topic, so I don't know anything about his message. Southern Ohio is a long way from Mecca. Where I came from the formula is simple. America, love it or leave it.

On February 21, 1965, three weeks before Malcolm X plans to join up with Dr. King in Selma and expand the network, he is assassinated in Harlem. All hush-hush in Hillsboro.

That summer in Watts, California, nine-year-old David Ornette Cherry—my future collaborator on *No Strangers Here Today* and *The Hillsboro Story*—walks out of his house. Two blocks away, tanks are rolling into his neighborhood. Police are beating his people. People are getting killed. "The Watts Riots," the papers scream, "black people going nuts." But in Watts, the people call it the Rebellion. The poets and musicians take to the streets, David remembers. The music never stops.

Class of '65. The prom, graduation, getting into college, partying before we all head out into life—it's all supposed to be fun.

Detroit Burns

Van Gogh's sunflowers over my walnut bed in my own bedroom, those days are over. I start college at Ohio University and live in a dorm that smells like cleaning supplies. I'm not cut out for fraternity parties or sorority teas. I go through the motions and take solace in studying zoology. I have my own cat to dissect. It is my first major peek into a system, albeit a dead system, devoid of feeling. I go to the lab and pull my cat out of the storage unit, assailed by the formaldehyde, feeling guilty about the cat. Still, I am fascinated. I can see where the organs are located, how the muscles move the skeleton, the mechanics, the muscle of the heart.

I go out for the diving team, where I quickly discover that the real competitors have been coached and are from Cleveland and Cincinnati. The OU diving coach is a very positive, upbeat man, what you'd expect from a diving coach, not that I have expectations. I am completely intimidated, but the upbeat coach, who knows I will not be going up against the big-league divers, works with me anyway to break a few of my bad habits before I quit. To wrap up the season, he rigs up a trapeze, flips upside down as the catcher, and gives each of us a turn at flying across the entire pool. I climb to the terrifying diving platform where the daredevils dive. My coach swings toward me. I have to let go, reach out and free fall. Have faith. Feel the timing. We lock wrists and pendulum through space, two bodies connected and free.

I study the New Deal in American history and begin to talk with my parents about their worlds, what they remember, the bank holiday, the Depression, the Fireside Chats, how my grandparents, Grace and Ira, sat in their living room next to the radio console and listened to FDR set out his vision for America, his economic bill of rights, more sweeping than the constitution. History comes alive through their stories.

In the spring, on April 4, 1967, Dr. King delivers the most powerful political speech of his career, "Beyond Vietnam,"[13] at Riverside Church in New York City. He expands his critique of the system to include class and foreign policy. He denounces the Vietnam War and calls America the "greatest purveyor of violence in the world.... There is nothing except a tragic death wish to prevent us from reordering our priorities, so that the pursuit of peace will take precedence over the pursuit of war." He lifts the veil of illusion. The *New York Times* calls the speech "a mistake." I don't hear it or read it or read about it. The words never arrive in my world. King has gone too far, people are saying. *Time, Newsweek*, they're ignoring him now.

That summer, 1967, urban ghettos in a hundred American cities explode, fueled by unemployment, poverty, the build-up in Vietnam, rage against social betrayal. The whole country is awake now. Tension explodes on the West Coast into the Summer of Love in San Francisco, The Jimi Hendrix Experience, tuning in and turning on a new social order.

I carry on in the old social order and get a summer job as a lifeguard at the Chillicothe Country Club where I can swim laps, practice my diving moves, work on my tan while on the job. The wealthy housewives stretch out on the reclining lawn chairs, gossip, rub Coppertone into their skin, smoke Salems, order club sandwiches from the kitchen, made and served by the Black help, read *Vogue* and *Redbook*.

Four hours north, Detroit burns for four days.

The Way In

Back at Ohio University for my last year, I sign up for a dance class to fill out my requirements for a PE major. The class is taught by Shirley Wimmer, who has just arrived at OU to start a dance department. She trained and performed with the techno-inventive choreographer Alwin Nikolais, whose roots went back to the German choreographer Mary Wigman, who studied how a finger moved, the engineering of the body, how curiosity could free movement from the tyranny of fairy tales and allow the body its full expression.

Shirley's training integrates technique, improvisation, and composition in the same class—action, exploration of action, invention with action—movement free of competition. I am back home with my natural language, coloring it, shaping it. Feelings locked into little corners under my skin find their way out into space through movement design and physical connection. Shirley is a dance ethnographer—she studied dance in India—and offers a global perspective, the spiritual and cultural roots of dance imagination. She opens the path to art. Dance is the way in.

Carl Jung's concept of the collective unconscious in my Bible as Literature class begins to puncture my perception bubble. Someone is yelling on the streets of Athens Ohio while I head for class. Martin Luther King has been killed.

On April 4, 1968, exactly one year after his powerful speech at Riverside Church, the prophet of non-violence is assassinated in Memphis, on the verge of launching his Poor People's Campaign. [14]

Two months later, Robert Kennedy, leading Presidential candidate who has just won the California primary, running against Richard Nixon on a platform to end the Vietnam War, is assassinated, another 'lone assassin,' another shock to the system, like a one-two punch from Muhammad Ali.

Next, Black Panther leader and community organizer, Fred Hampton, a rising star from Chicago, is gunned down mafia style in his bed while sleeping next to his pregnant partner.

My soul is shaken and I start to look—the violence, the war, the vets coming back with their stories, the string of assassinations with suspicious cover-ups, the systematic delivery of the economy to giant multi-nationals moving operations out of the country to escape labor unions—it's all there to see.

The revolutionaries are painting the picture with their bodies on the line. The journalists are writing and photographing the stories. The musicians and poets are drumming up the spirits. I start to feel the movement, sense the bigger dance, and awkwardly begin to lurch toward a dream out there on horizon—a little hazy, but, oh well, I'll figure it out.

ELSEWHERE
1970

A story's choreography is global and geographic when you step back and look at life this way—how you circle around and have chance encounters, how your life starts to take a shape, how, little by little, your blues hit the heat of imagination and you are somewhere else.

Look, there I am, twenty years old, with a confused vision of a house with a picket fence and fun adventures Elsewhere, and I marry Garry Boone in the summer of '68. He was my boyfriend in the fifth grade. He threw notes to me out the window of the school bus as it went by. He has a big imagination. I am correcting my golf swing.

Fortunately, I have seen my first Fellini film, and the strange people in *Juliet of the Spirits* have captured my imagination, but for now, I am stuck in a trailer park on the outskirts of Athens, Ohio trying to cook a pot roast. You have to start somewhere.

Garry and I get teaching jobs with the Beaverton School District, near Portland, Oregon. Recruiters are looking for good Midwest stock to counterbalance the edgy effects of the social revolution creeping up the West Coast. We hitch the U-Haul up to my Pontiac Le Mans, point the car west, step on the accelerator, away from the status quo, toward a new world.

There I am in my Bermuda shorts, the PE teacher at Aloha High School, an experiment in progressive education. Garry is assigned to Beaverton High School, a traditional school where he is the high school drama teacher. At Aloha, we are required to start the year with sensitivity training to become more attuned to each other as faculty members. I am introduced to Fritz Pearls and Gestalt theory and "active listening." What a concept.

Fritz Pearls: "What we say is mostly either lies or bullshit. But the voice is there, the gesture, the postures, the facial expression, the psychosomatic language. It's all there if you learn to more or less to let the content play the second violin. And if you don't make the mistake of mixing up sentences and reality and you use your eyes and ears, then you see that everyone expresses himself one way or another... the world is open. Nobody can have any secrets because the neurotic only fools himself, nobody else, except for awhile, maybe, if he's a good actor."[15]

On the first day of sensitivity training, I meet Rosemary, the typing teacher, who has red nails, a red sports car, five boyfriends, a fondue pot, good weed, and opinions. Rosie and I laugh so hard, I am born again. We push the limits of the educational experiment and trade places one day. I teach typing and Rosie is out there with a whistle. We roller skate into the faculty meeting, where all decisions are made by consensus.

The faculty are fascinating. An English teacher and her husband live in the caretaker's house at Pittock Mansion, the landmark estate of the first newspaper publisher in Portland, with panoramic views of the mountains surrounding the city of Portland. Pat, another English teacher, an Ernest Hemmingway type, takes Rosie and me hunting. He drives us out to the gold and green canyons in the high desert, near the wheat farms of Eastern Oregon with the wide blue skies. We are supposed to rustle up wild turkeys and kill them with guns he gives us. But we go back to the car and get stoned instead.

Two social studies teachers—Jim, the descendant of early Oregon pioneers and Merle, fit and lively—lead us up to the top of Mt. Hood. We leave the massive fireplaces in the majestic Timberline Lodge and start up before dawn. The crevasses are terrifying. We put on crampons, rope up at the end to the skinny mountaintop with a view of the Cascades below us, Three Sisters, Mt. St. Helens, Mt. Adams, the whole world.

There's Garry driving off. We have decided to split up over hamburgers. There isn't much to discuss. We're not Julie Christie and Omar Sharif in *Dr. Zhivago*, that's for sure. He gets the TV set and Romulus, the beagle. I don't know what happened to Remus, the other beagle. I didn't even know they were twins in Roman mythology. Oh well... I get the stereo.

There I am, calling in sick, putting on my new George Harrison album and sewing a yellow dress. I am free as a bird. I've had my first opinion!

Rosie and I are digging razor clams at the coast, driving to Baha through Sausalito so Rosie can hook up with her fireman boyfriend, listening to Neil Young, making plans after we quit our jobs to go see the world.

Rosie joins the Peace Corps and is assigned to Kenya. I don't even know where Kenya is on the map of Africa.

IF IT AIN'T
GOT THAT SWING

Believing seems to me to belong to that vague feeling in which I recognize myself. Expectation. But if you ask me what I expect, I can't answer you.

Federico Fellini

CAUGHT
HILLSBORO, MAY, 2003

A lightning bolt strikes the four-hundred-year-old oak tree in front of Hillsboro High School the night Philip Partridge dies, May 19, 2003—like the strike of a match. Boom.

I arrive in Hillsboro the next day to begin the investigation and am standing next to the toppled giant, wondering what Philip Partridge is trying to say.

Body first.

I am location scouting, feeling my way through the landscape, like an actor in a movie, like the cinematographer, the art director. My body knows these alleys, the pond, the fields, the sounds and smells. My body is remembering. My body perks up every time I pass a house on North High Street.

I stop in at the library to read the documents Mrs. Goodrich has copied for me.

Hillsboro Press Gazette, *October, 1954*:

The sheriff went to the Partridge house on North High Street about 7:15 a.m. The engineer had not yet arisen. After breakfast and after he had read the commitment order, he gathered his clothes, and accompanied on the trip by his wife, a registered nurse, went along "willingly," officers said. Partridge offered little comment on the matter, they added.

I jot the address down from a newspaper article to locate the house. It's the house that has been calling to me. I'm listening.

Philip Partridge, in *If It Ain't Got That Swing*: "A century before it had been a tavern they said. Walls three bricks thick, anchored together at the second-floor level with tie bars, white fence, post and cross pieces like the Kentucky horse farms, a fulsome growth of plants and trees, and the shade of giant overhanging maples, all on a gentle slope. We loved it."

You caught me.

WINDY HILL
OCTOBER, 2003

Tom Partridge, the oldest son of Philip and Elizabeth, is showing me around his two-hundred-acre farm on Route 73, ten miles from Hillsboro. He named it *Windy Hill*. We drive down a steep dirt lane to Tom's dream-house-in-progress, made from massive two-hundred-year-old wood beams and siding from barns in Kentucky. He designed the house from sketches on a paper napkin, a stately vision—historic, rustic, elegant.

The covered front porch faces fields of horses, old barns, a windmill, a pond, herons with weathervane hats. Dogs run free. White oaks and maples are quaking and shaking their October oranges, reds, and golds off into windy skies. Green metal bouncy lawn chairs, like my grandparents sat in on Sunday afternoons, wait in the side yard for new paint. Fences need mending. Cows plod toward the barn, eternally saturated in musty smells of animal earth life.

"This is my legacy," Tom says.

We head up to the old original farmhouse to do the interview. Tom is headstrong, freethinking, easy laughing, a thoroughbred who loves Bob Marley. He converted the glassed-in, light-filled porch into a stylish oral surgery office, where he takes a day off from his practice in Cincinnati to perform root canals while patients watch cows chew their cud. The waiting room, with its handsome leather chairs and *Architectural Digest*s, leads into the farm kitchen and then into the living room where I meet Tom's mother, Elizabeth Partridge, propped up in a daybed. Tom moved his parents to *Windy Hill* as they became more physically challenged.

Elisabeth is frail, "like a bird," Tom says. Her voice is delicate, her thoughts simply stated. Her nails are painted bright pink. Her ninety-three-year-old smile is holy and gold-leafed. My eyes scan the living room and settle on a framed photograph on the mantel. Elizabeth is wearing a black suit with shoulder pads and good lines, a white blouse with spattered designs, unbuttoned at the top in a v-line, white pearls. Her hair is stylishly cropped, earrings are pearl, big round glasses, vintage '60s. Her handsome husband, Philip, is wearing a white suit and looking straight at the camera with a terrific smile. Her eyes look slightly off to the right of the camera. Something has caught her attention. Her smile is solid, matches his energy. Is it happiness? Elizabeth and Philip are leaning in towards each other. His arm is around her.

His hand is on her back.

She feels the gentle pressure through her suit.

Timely Letters

Tom: "When he came back from prison, his county engineer's job was gone. People wanted him to go back and run for the office, but he couldn't because of his conviction. He was really qualified for some terrific jobs."

Philip Partridge: "After my release on parole, though scrambling around like mad in the contracting and surveying business to rescue my family's desperate financial situation, I still managed to write timely letters on public affairs."

"Dear Reverend Boughton:

It is a matter of deep concern that Reverend Maurice McCrackin is under threat of dismissal from his church and from the Presbyterian Church for his refusal to pay federal taxes that support our vast military structure.

The economies of our time have fallen under the domination of military industrial combines that pose an increasing threat to the safety of our world. These self-perpetuating conglomerates with their political connections have a vested interest in producing ever more ferocious weapons that no power seems able to stop.

Reverend McCrackin deserves the highest praise for putting one man's life—his own—above the pursuit of comforts and plaudits of the marketplace.

It is not appropriate that in a country of our traditions, a man of such high principles who serves God by defying the machinery of death should suffer punishment by his own church.

Respectfully yours,
Philip H. Partridge"

Then There was Ed Davis

Tom: "We went to Florida for a year. Dad worked at Cape Canaveral. We came back here, and I graduated in '59. Then later they moved to New Mexico. My brother spent his senior year out there, graduated, Four Corners, New Mexico. Mom worked on a Pueblo up there in Four Corners, in public health."

Elizabeth: "We didn't stay but a year. He got a job as City Engineer in Akron. We lived there four years."

Akron, memoir

Philip: "One Sunday I sought out and went to a black peoples' church in a poor section of the city. The date is indelibly fixed in history. Four little girls were killed by a bomb blast in a Birmingham black peoples' church the same day, the same hour. The coincidence was astonishing. I had not gone to a black peoples' church in twelve years.

"I became an activist in the New Politics League and started screaming letters against the Viet Nam War. President Ike had sent advisors. That was bad enough. JFK was sending troops. And that was worse.

"When I started getting haircuts at Tom Sistrunk's Co-op Barber Shop on Main Street, I was not fanning the flames of revolution. Conversation was lively, always friendly. The haircuts were excellent. Tom asked me to run for President of CORE (*Congress of Racial Equality*). Instincts said no. What if some of the black people turned against me. This would break my heart. It has happened a time or two.

"Then there was Ed Davis, a tennis player, President of the City Employees Union, a warm and unforgettable black man. He had never finished second grade, worked at a car wash for a decade or two. I invited him to speak to our Toastmaster Club. He declined to stand before us, but sat among us, a father figure, gentle, wise, the greatest man in town.

"Someone suggested getting up a class intended to help black people and white people communicate. I dodged this completely. I could think of nothing so stultifying as a course in how to communicate with black people. The way to communicate is to get into projects and work to a common goal. I promoted a yard games festival for CORE at the downtown city park. Volleyball, badminton, horseshoes, dart throwing, basket shooting, Frisbee throwing. It was delightful. Good participation. Black people and white people playing together."

Not My Concern

Tom: "I think there's a huge invisible barrier. It's very interesting. Everybody talks about their black friends, and I don't have any black friends that come to my house, and I don't know any white people, almost any, who do. And I think the reverse is true.

"Cincinnati has its own unique sense of barriers and has had for a long time. It's an old German town and a lot of that mentality runs stuff and is still there. None of the Jewish businessmen, no matter how successful they were, could get in to the local men's clubs. They actually created a club, which, I think burned down. Either by accident or by...

(pause)

"... probably by accident; they created a club, called it The Phoenix, 1930 or '40.

"Marge Schott... she owned the Cincinnati Reds for years... carried Nazi flags. About four years ago the big organization in baseball basically squeezed her out. She was an embarrassment. She chain smoked. You're not allowed to smoke in the stadium. Well, she was the owner, sat right behind home plate, and here are the cameras on her and she's smoking. In some magazine, she said, 'Well Hitler did some good y'know.'

"A guy named Carl Lindner—very right wing, pseudo-Christian—he controls the *Enquirer*. Nobody says much. I haven't heard anybody say anything anti-Semitic, but... it's strange. I think it's an odd thing. I don't know what's going on with all that. Is it overt hatred? No. Just nobody wants to deal with it. Not my concern."

Toastmasters

Akron, memoir

Philip: "Most of the Toastmasters members were Good-year engineers, highly educated and articulate. But they were generally complacent, conformists. I gradually decided to drop a 'bomb' on them.... I gathered material from things I'd read that were provocative, not pleasant but true. All in my head, nothing written down.... I opened by citing some of the unfavorable facts of the domestic scene. Top of the world in suicide, crime, accidents, divorce, insanity, alcoholism, drug addiction, unemployment, corruption in high places, high illiteracy rate, twenty percent of the population doomed to perpetual poverty.

"I told them that the Diems maintained a ruthless repression of the eighty percent Buddhist Vietnamese people, graft and nepotism everywhere, a hideous mockery of freedom. That Cardinal Thuc of the Diem family had amassed some three hundred million dollars trafficking in gambling, narcotics and prostitution as reported in a leading international newspaper.

"In the old days in frontier towns of the west, when life got so monotonous that people couldn't stand each other, the roughnecks in town would catch a stray dog, douse him with kerosene, and set fire to his tail. And he'd liven things up for a while. Now we drop bombs and napalm on civilian populations so that nobody knows how many thousands, including women and children, are maimed and slowly burned to death.

"Next day at work I awaited the verdict. It had been a rough speech. But the roof hadn't fallen in. Maybe I had been wrong about things. In the middle of the afternoon a fellow

Toastmaster phoned me at work. 'It was a fine speech… needed to be said… congratulations.'

"But something happened. By suppertime I was having trouble passing urine. Never before in my fifty-two years. By bed time it was thick with blood. The next day I spent in bed with a severe 'kidney infection,' stayed there five days, fever 104 degrees. Instant reflex.

"I had deliberately walked into this one.

"When the reflex immediately follows a challenge, so that the probability of coincidence is like one in a million or less, you are pretty sure you have something. When you get two instant reflexes, or three, you know you are hitting the ball. This narrative is loaded with dozens of them.

"Anyone with even a rudimentary knowledge of modern physics knows that high frequency sound waves or laser beams, and heaven knows what else, can punish and kill at a considerable distance by remote control.

"Seven days later the Diems were overthrown and murdered. Twenty-eight days later President Kennedy was assassinated.

"One thing for sure. The 'lone assassin' yarn that history is trying to digest is phony as a seven-dollar bill."

We Out Lived 'Em

Tom: Then they went to New York, Manhattan.

Elizabeth: Seventeen years. We lived on Columbia Street.

Tom: East Side. Not far from Hell's Kitchen. Lower East Side.

Elizabeth: We could see across the East River from our place. Queens, Brooklyn. All the way up and down the river. We were seventeen floors up. I liked living in New York.

Tom: They became very much city people

Elizabeth: I was a nurse for forty years before I quit. I worked at Bellevue. I just went on the bus every morning to Bellevue Hospital and then home in the afternoon. They had public health office in the building, along with everything. They have a big psychiatry portion of the hospital too. That's what most people think it is, but they have more general patients than they do psychiatry patients. It's a big hospital.

Tom: She was in public health. She dealt with county people here in Highland County, then worked at Bellevue, which is the biggest public health center in the world. She would go out and take care of people in the direst of circumstances.

Elizabeth: A bunch of the girls got to going to the ballet, and we had season tickets and from work we'd take our clothes to work and dress and go out to dinner and then go to the ballet. I had lots of fun there.

Tom: My father was always involved in things there. He was always volunteering to set up athletic programs, tournaments, three-on-three basketball, track meets—he did all kinds of stuff—in his neighborhood.

Elizabeth: He was a painter. He had an exhibit in New York at the Board of Education, downtown New York.

Tom: They were pictures of New York. Construction pictures. World Trade Center. They were pretty interesting I think.

Elizabeth: He was the Chief engineer on the largest building ever built by Bell Telephone Company. It's uptown. 5th Avenue and... I think it's Madison.

Tom: It's a monster building.

Elizabeth: Most of our friends are gone now. We outgrew 'em, outlived 'em.

Was It Magic, Was It Love?

Philip Partridge: "When I visited Ted Lewis in the summer of 1986, he reminisced about a number of things. I remembered his grocery, always neat, immaculate, the best-kept store in town. He told how he had sold his store and bought a farm, trained and ran race horses. But he was now retired. He spoke with pride of the achievements of his three children, now grown, well situated with families of their own.

"He recounted tales of the protest days. For seeking to enroll his children in the white public school, he had been arrested and locked up. Then they went to his mother. 'If you will mortgage your home and put up bail, we will release him.' to which Ted immediately replied, 'Mama. Don't you *ever* mortgage your house.'

"He was released after a time. Segregated schools remained. Half the black people in town shunned him, he said. Thought he was a communist. Ted never complained. But this must have hurt his business.

"There was something about the little black people's church. Was it magic? Was it love? Was it God? Did it matter? Rev. Burr, the white-topped, blind preacher who shuttled between half a dozen small town churches. Dignity, patience, gentle manners, always the right words, unflappable. I contrasted them with my own inept communications at times. I had never been in close association with black people before.

"Ernest and Marion Bromley. Elsie McCoy, a land-wealthy Quaker lady. "Hammie," proprietor of the off-campus lunch counter. Ted Lewis. And I. We were a team of seven. Dedicated but alone. Our activities consisted mainly of holding regular meetings, drawing up petitions to the School Board and writing letters."

You Can Always Hear Music

Tom: "He was in his room there. We had a house full of people. We told people they'd better come, the kids and stuff. They told us he only had a few days. I went to see him and he was kind of struggling breathing with his eyes closed. And I told him, 'Dad, everyone's in the next room, we're having dinner. As soon as we're finished, I'll be right back in.' I patted him and he did a little nod like that. We're in there chittering and chattering and making noise eating and I come back out and he was gone."

Ann Richter, Philip's sister: "I was down in Hillsboro when my brother passed on. The night that he passed on, there was a big storm and a huge old oak tree in the school yard blew down. Of course that sounds sort of superstitious, but that's a fact. I was impressed by that, but I don't know if it would make any difference to anybody else, but it seemed kind of significant to me."

Beth Partridge, Philip's Granddaughter: "I drove them every year back and forth from Michigan to Florida. Oh, I cherish that time in the car…you talk. Grandma would have her Statler Brothers tape of the old gospel songs and all three of us would just sing them through the mountains [laughing]. Grandpa would do the bass, you know. He'd whistle, and he thought that was the greatest thing. I remember I was just whistling once. 'You know, if you whistle you can always hear music, you can always play music.' That's what he said. He was so tickled that I could whistle. All of a sudden, I'm a genius."

THE SHADOW PLAY

Memory is a mysterious element that links us to things we don't even remember having lived. But it constantly incites us to stay in contact with dimensions, with events, sensations we can't define but that we know actually happened.

Federico Fellini

BLUE NOTE

The system was weak to begin with, the planters building on the death cult of slavery, genocide, war. The roots are weak, and the parasites have grown more virulent.

The people in the play pushed the system, tried to correct the system's imbalances, and you don't see their faces in the history books. They were scorned, fired from jobs, sent to prison, ignored, threatened, beaten up, called crazy and uppity. They weren't trying to be heroes. They were swept into the events as children, spouses, emissaries of the system. They all had ordinary lives.

All of the people in this story are alive with energy and history and contour. This story is not about small-town drama, although drama drives the story. The story is about power, about who controls memory, who has the authority to speak.

White history and black history are different histories. The memory of the native people in Highland County is different from the memory of descendants of settlers. Men and women feel memory in different detail. Rich people have different locations for their memories than poor people. Short people see things differently than tall people. Fresh minds translate memory. Stuck minds cling to memory.

Trauma locks down memory. Movement breaks memory open.

Action heals. The dance heals.

Think of this as a family story. This is our family. This is what they have to tell us about our family.

Bell's Opera House
Hillsboro, Ohio

Mom is entering from stage right. 1933, sixteen years old, wearing a dark blue pleated skirt down to her calves, stylish white blouse with a round collar, sensible shoes, hair parted to the side, slight curl. She and her fellow musicians have traveled from their village of Mowrystown, fifteen miles away, to perform at Bell's Opera House. She steps into the blue spotlight and begins her trumpet solo. Look at her. She's so nervous her knees are knocking.

Bell's Opera House, the uptown vaudeville hall that can seat a thousand people, is the regional center of entertainment—high school variety shows, traveling theatre companies, local talent, campaign speeches, silent movies, then the talkies. Actors have sturdy attitudes and vocal stamina. Colored people have to sit in the upper balcony.

Si and Lenora Gordon—Connie's parents—buy the building in the early '50s. Si opens Gordon's Auto Supply on the street level, stocked with fan belts, flexible flyers, widgets, ratchets. The opera house takes up the second and third floors of the building—a chunk of the city block—but it is too run down to renovate, so the ghosts of the theatre sit around collecting dust. We are never allowed to go up there—too dirty, too delicate, too dangerous.

Fifty years later the Gordon girls inherit Bell's Opera House and put the building on the market to settle the estate. The town buzzes with opinions about the price. There are visions of renovating the old vaudeville hall into a historic site and regional arts center, attracting tourism to the region. Connie suggests I contact the realtor and go through Bell's

Opera House on my next trip to Hillsboro to work on the story. Finally, I will see this mysterious space that holds the sounds of my mother's trumpet. I don't know why, but that seems important.

The realtor who meets me at Bells Opera House to show me around is an attractive woman with a vast mane of brown hair and an easy, gracious manner, Risa Boone.

"Are you, by any chance, married to Garry Boone?" I knew he was back in town.

"Yes, I'm married to Garry. You were his favorite ex-wife."

We laugh and light shafts into the theatre through the long dusty windows. She knows I am not going to buy the opera house, but wants to explore too—this vast creaky wooden structure, drafty and dreamlike, hazardous and combustible. The big oak office cupboard still holds old tickets and programs and booklets of the Constitution for the patrons, written before the Nineteenth Amendment, before the ladies were citizens.

Curtains are weighted down with decades of dust. Lights and props, ropes and pulleys are piled up backstage. The backdrop for the stage is a faded painting of a woman standing alone on the veranda of a villa, one hand on her heart, the other resting on the stone wall, looking out toward the landscape in a pose of longing, forever longing.

A director's chair sits below the stage. I sit down in the chair and imagine Mom's trumpet sounds bouncing through the space. *Willow Weep for Me.*

Risa walks over and says, "Garry would love to see you."

I'm hanging out in the driveway of their home and Garry is telling me how he made his way back to Hillsboro after living in Hollywood, writing for *Happy Days,* starting businesses, several wives and children.

I tell him about my project.

"I have Philip Partridge's memoir," he says.

Philip Partridge wrote a memoir?

The Partridge family hired Garry to help Philip edit the memoir. Garry always wanted to make a movie of the Philip Partridge story.

"Can you make me a copy right now?"

"Sure." No hesitation. We jump into his dented silver '81 RX7 convertible and head up highway 73 to the school where he teaches English to at-risk youth. He opens a file cabinet, pulls out the document, and photocopies the entire three-hundred-and-fifty-page manuscript, *If It Ain't Got That Swing,* complete with his edits.

The pages spit out of the machine. I feel like Nancy Drew on acid. I don't know what to say. He's been working on a novel for twenty-five years, based on memories of growing up in Hillsboro. He asks me if I want to read it and I say no, and ask him who his favorite writer is, and he says William Kennedy, and then he says he trusts me, which surprises me, and then the machine stops, and he hands me the memoir.

Is this why I married Garry Boone? Did I marry Garry to bring me to this moment?

"You know," Garry looks at me, "Philip Partridge was crazy."

PRIME CUT
UPTOWN HILLSBORO, THE NEXT DAY

Tom Partridge: "I can't believe you were married to that asshole."

Tom and I are at the Prime Cut for rib-eyes and cocktails. I want to tell him in person that I have Philip's memoir because Garry Boone copied it for me. Tom is furious and goes on and on about what a jerk Garry is. The family told him to never copy the manuscript. Something went on during editing sessions that upset Philip, so the family fired Garry. Trying to decipher the editing, I would have fired Garry too. But that's not the point. "So where is the original manuscript?"

"It burned up in the fire," he says. The fire that consumed Tom's first dream house, the one he sketched out on a cocktail napkin. Someone left a combustible container near the fireplace, and the house burned to the ground—heirlooms, documents, objects, clothes, everything, gone.

"So if Garry had listened to you, the memoir would be gone. If I hadn't married Garry Boone, I would not have the memoir. We wouldn't be here now. I'm glad I married Garry. Is it okay with you if I work with the memoir?"

I don't know what I mean exactly, except that this changes everything, but Tom seems to trust me, and I promise to send him all my drafts. "Your dad was a good writer, his voice, like Sherwood Anderson." I'm thinking of *Winesburg, Ohio,* the eccentric characters living in a small town in Ohio, each with a peculiar truth about life.

Tom: "His parents were educators and doctors. He was a thoughtful guy. He saw what was going on a long time ago— the level of corruption. The promise was always democracy. America. The Constitution and Democracy. The Elites.

They hate democracy. They hate public education. They hate higher education. They have feudal estates. These so-called Christians are very similar to radical Islamists. Here they've had the same opportunity to find out how democracy works, and they're oblivious.

"We have a recent Clermont County Commissioner who always had his photograph taken with a full head-shot of Jesus. He just got caught taking drugs over to young girls in Kentucky and buying sex and having them masturbate on drugs. Archie Wilson. He was one of the champions of the Tea Party people. He's kind of classic—always had his photo taken with a picture of Jesus.

"If you create fear, all the time in the media—look at Rupert Murdock. He came here to create a media phenomenon that warps peoples' perception of reality, on a multi-national level. BP loves him. Banks love him. Big drug companies love him.

"The apathy of the wealthy elite. That really bothers me. They're all scared. They used to have some influence. They don't now."

Tom pauses. I don't have much to say. He's said it all.

The check comes and Tom picks it up, leaves a twenty-dollar tip, and walks me to my rental car. "I think there's something going on that's bigger than us," I say to Tom.

"I think so too," he replies.

In the dream Tom and I are discussing investments and he advises me, "No, not stocks. Poetry."

REMOTE CONTROL TORTURE
MID-'70s

Philip Partridge: "At a question and answer period following a speech on Civil Rights by distinguished columnist Carl Rowan, I stood up and stated that I had been subjected to severe tortures of kidneys and heart by invisible weapons in response to my protests over the Viet Nam War. Rowen, black, ignored my statement as though I were some kind of a nut and went on to the next question.

"Numerous appeals to other groups were brushed aside. *Amnesty International*—concerned about foreign torture, but not at home. *People for the American Way*—feeble response, then dropped it. *Americans United for Separation of Church and State.* No answer. *Southern Poverty Law Center*, no answer. *United Negro College Fund*, likewise.

"A personal appeal to Editor McWilliams of that great socialist paper, *The Nation.* A smirking grin. Letters to the Press—Clayton Fritchey, Harriett Van Horne, Mary McCrory, Drew Pearson of the *New York Post.* The first three came up with concerned replies asking, in effect, what proof did I have. Well, what proof do I have? That's what this documentary is all about. Pearson wrote a column, almost quoting from my letter and leading to speculation that further disclosures would follow. Within a week he was dead.

"I went to Washington where Senator Frank Church's Committee was investigating espionage and other official atrocities in our country against freedom. Each day for three days I left notes briefly stating the problem and asking for a hearing. No acknowledgement.

"Secret torture by remote control. Not that they couldn't do it, for this is evident to any half-way student of modern physics. But that secret agents would do it to punish and intimidate a private citizen for expressing unorthodox ideas. How gigantic was it?

"The following are evidences, separate incidents that occurred over a period of three years, often weeks or months apart, and not in chronological order. Five times as many I have forgotten. I didn't write them down until the end of the Akron experience because I didn't want to inhibit the action. The 'eyes' and 'ears' were on me every second."

COUP
WINDY HILL, 2006

Joe Partridge: "He always felt that he was being listened to and our phones were being tapped. Ever since the '54 incidents."

Joe is the younger son of Philip and Elizabeth Partridge, a retired Colonel living in Texas. He began his military career in the Special Forces, Green Beret, then became a dentist and professor, designed whole dental offices to be dropped into combat zones.

What about war? The Iraq War is exposed—the torture, the traumatized people, Exxon Mobil showing record profits, the lies about weapons of mass destruction. He is inside the culture. What do the generals think?

Joe: "They all hate Rumsfeld. He's actually insane. They're going to drop all these high- tech bombs from the sky and people throw up their arms and surrender. Of course, this has always failed. Never worked. High tech stuff may change the way you implement war, but basically war is a human relations thing. This is a total failure."

"Don't the generals take an oath to first protect the Constitution? Isn't your job to uphold the law? Geneva conventions. Who's stopping the torture and the insanity?"

Joe: "Military people are there to obey orders. You are not in a position to express your political views. That's the basic American military. But Chain of Command has broken down. The mission now is to make as much money as possible to satisfy the stockholders—Haliburton, Kellogg, Root and Brown, Khaki, Blackwater. Now the Pentagon is for sale. Now you have twenty different contractors answering to twenty different corporations and stockholders. When the shit hits the fan, who's going to fix the helicopter? Who's going to fly the mission? What is the mission? Unity of command is completely blown out."

Joe and are I sitting in the living room of Tom's second dream house. After the first dream house burned down, Tom started over, hired the same Mennonite carpenters, found more old barn beams in Kentucky, more antiques, built another massive fireplace is the center of a living room with sitting nooks, leather couches, long dining room table, well-stocked kitchen, veranda. I feel like Elizabeth Taylor in the ranch house in the movie "Giant," with James Dean and Rock Hudson, set in Texas oil fields, the backdrop to the great American power dance.

"What incidents in '54?" I ask.

"My last year in high school, before we moved, I had my learner's permit. He needed to take the car down the road to a mechanic. We were in the house and he said, 'Can you take it down?' I said, 'Dad I just have my learner's permit.' 'Well, it's just down there six blocks.' 'Well, okay Pops, if it's only six blocks.' So I got in the car and he came out and says, 'Maybe I'd better go with you.' We went down the road, and right there they had a police blockade checking all the cars and license plates. I'd never seen a police blockade. Later I asked Tommy Hogsett—he was in the police department—I just kind of ask him, casually, 'Do you guys ever do routine traffic stops for citizens?' 'No, we never do that.' "

"So what do you make of that?"

"J. Edgar Hoover and his crowd. Paranoia is based on seeds and fact. I have no doubt, you know, that… J. Edgar Hoover was notorious… I'm sure he was bugging the telephone. But this wasn't on the phone."

"So your house was bugged?"

"I don't think there's any question about it. The statistical odds of that thing of that happening on that afternoon on one isolated street, I mean it has to be in one in a billion billion, as Carl Sagan says. So that probably started the seeds of paranoia."

Philip Partridge: "I am writing the history for a week, living alone in the 'privacy' of our cottage nine miles north of Saugatuck (Michigan). Each time I return to the cottage after dark, the door was not only unlocked, but ajar. The restaurant proprietess—Catholic. Vatican mafia everywhere. No escape."

Joe: "I have no idea. I don't know what was on his mind in his later years. Paranoia is a seed that starts it. After that, it grows wild. I have no idea..."

"Sounds like Godfather III—who he was pointing at, how they work, who they work for...."

Joe: "We now have the greatest corporate mafia ever in the history of mankind running this economy. When I was in Special Operations, we trained people to do subtle sabotage—go into a country, do a mission for six months, come out, never fire a shot and complete our mission because we did things subtly.

"Basically I look at this as corporate Special Operations on the government of the United States. They have come in and basically taken over our government and drained it of its blood and the American people don't know what the hell happened."

"That's a coup."

Joe: "It is! Absolutely it is. Make no mistake. There is a shadow government running this country. It could almost be written in a Special Operations book."

THE TECHNIQUE OF THE BIG LIE
1965

Philip Partridge: "One evening the newscasts carried a stinging blast from Dean Rusk, our usually mild Secretary of State, at the East European countries for refusing to pay their dues toward the UN peace keeping operations in the Congo. I wrote the Secretary recalling the circumstances, that Moise Tshombe, the appointee of the reactionary capitalists who tried to split Katanga off from the Congo, had thrown Lumumba, the elected President, in prison from which he soon 'escaped' to be promptly murdered as the Russians predicted he would be. And that when Hammarskjöld was returning from his investigation of the incident, which would likely blow the lid off the whole affair, his plane had crashed killing all aboard. And that some foreign papers had reported that the plane was found to have been carrying three thousand pounds of explosives. And that a U.S. Marine bodyguard who miraculously survived for twenty-four hours had said there were six separate explosions that tore the plane apart. And that no word of this had ever appeared in the American press or newscasts. And that under the circumstances, it was scarcely surprising that Eastern European countries had refused to help pay for the operation.

"The letter was never answered. But it produced three astonishing 'instant reflexes' as I called them. The morning I mailed it, I was seized with an angina pectoris type of heart pressure, very painful, that nearly K-O'd me. I quickly left the office and walked the streets for an hour taking in all the oxygen I could handle. It gradually subsided and I returned to work.

"The same day evidence of the black underground communication network surfaces again. Malcolm X issued a statement as reported in the news media saying the same things my letter had said about the UN Congo operation and the murder of Lumumba and Hammarskjöld. The next day Malcolm X was murdered, by black men of course. The technique of the big lie."

BLUE NOTE

I am a child of the Cold War, molded by the bell curve, scripted for the good life, silenced by practicality. Africa was impractical and primitive and needed help, lots of help from us, the winners who lived at the top of the bell curve, the ones who grew the economies.

A child of the frozen Cold War feels the war against nature, against her own instinctual dreaming nature. The Cold War belittles dreamers. You are supposed to surrender your voice to civilization. Shhhh… Otherwise, you are an embarrassment.

The marching mothers were out on the streets to protect their children, not the American way of life.

The Cold War is a death cult. The cult has conducted eighty coups since 1953 when the U.S. State Department and the CIA merged operations. The coup in the Congo was the fifth.

I come to this story to rescue my child from the frozen Cold War, recover what I felt but could not name. The people in this story are guiding the retrieval. They are naming things.

REINVENTION
FEBRUARY, 2011, REED COLLEGE, PORTLAND, OREGON

Dr. Manning Marable, Director of the Center for Contemporary Black History at Columbia University, is a keynote speaker during Black History month. His twenty-year opus—*Malcolm X/A Life of Reinvention*—will be released in April and shed further light on the assassination of Malcolm X. I read that he had been ill and attribute a flat, academic lecture to a lack of vitality. Where was the spirit of Malcolm X?

I email him after the lecture with my "pressing questions" raised in Philip Partridge's memoir, pointing to the murder of Patrice Lumumba, Dag Hammarskjöld, and Malcolm X on the same page, as the "technique of the big lie." He writes back on February 28, 2011.

"Dear Susan,

Just a quick note of thanks for your recent email. Your timing expressed in your paragraph regarding Lumumba and Malcolm X is not quite right. Lumumba was murdered by white mercenaries in early 1961. When the news broke about Lumumba's death in February 1961, there were large demonstrations all over the world, but especially in New York City at the UN. Malcolm was still a member of the nation of Islam and he did not take direct part in these demonstrations. However, three years later, in 1964, Malcolm spent six months traveling throughout Africa and became very involved in efforts to help revolutionaries in the Congo, who had been supporters of Lumumba. Malcolm met with Che Guevara in 1964 and assisted him in planning his efforts to launch a military campaign in the Eastern Congo against the reactionaries and Europeans. Malcolm also spoke to the parliaments in Ghana, Kenya, and in other African countries to promote the cause of revolutionary Pan-Africanism. Malcolm was murdered on 21 February 1965, over four years after Lumumba was killed. Hopefully, these details will be helpful to you.

Sincerely yours,

Manning Marable"

WE ARE YOUR MONKEYS NO MORE

Marable's book barely mentions Patrice Lumumba. *Who Killed Hammarskjöld? The UN, the Cold War, and White Supremacy* by Susan Williams closes in on the "technique of the big lie." The following is a synopsis of her recent exposé:[16]

By 1960, sixteen African states had joined the United Nations, including the new Republic of Congo, which declared independence from Belgium in 1960, and in the first national elections ever held in the Congo, elected Patrice Lumumba as Prime Minister. The global balance of power was shifting.

Lumumba was a brilliant African leader emerging from the freedom movements worldwide, inspired by the Pan African vision of Kwame Nkrumah, founding member of the African Organization of Unity. Lumumba spent years educating himself and building a movement to reclaim the country for his people and re-build the social commonwealth.

The West found him distasteful. The Cold War moved its shadow operations to the rich mineral reserves located in the heart of Africa. Uranium for America's first atomic bomb came from the Congo. Losing the Congo was not an option. Lumumba, Eisenhower said, should be "eliminated."

During the inaugural celebrations, Belgium's King Baudouin's farewell address praised the Colonialists' contribution to the Congo and challenged the Congolese to show that they were worthy of their independence.

Patrice Lumumba stood up after the King had spoken: "No Congolese worthy of the name will be able to forget that this independence has been won through a struggle from day to day in which we did not spare our energy or our blood... We shall make the Congo a shining example for all of Africa... We are your monkeys no more."[17]

Two months later a military coup engineered by the CIA erupted in the capital. Parliament was dissolved. The military split Katanga Province—rich in minerals—off from the rest of the Congo, and Union Miniere, the Belgium mining conglomerate, installed the inexperienced young colonel named Joseph-Desiree Mobutu, groomed by the CIA, to command the country's military in Katanga.

Violence escalated, provoked by mercenaries, white supremacist death squads, and armed insurgents trained by American, Belgium, Rhodesian, and British special forces. Kasai province, dominated by a Belgian diamond mining conglomerate, broke off from the Congo, further devastating the economy.

Lumumba lost faith in the UN, too sluggish to halt the violence. Out of desperation, he appealed to the Soviet Union to supply weapons. "We are not Communists or Catholics," Lumumba proclaimed. "We are African Nationalists."

In January 1961, Patrice Lumumba was kidnapped, taken to a prison in Katanga, tortured, executed, cut into pieces, and buried in an unmarked location.

Che Guevara addressed the UN that December and described the dynamics of neocolonialism as 'military and economic collaboration' between Western powers.

'All free men in the world should prepare to avenge the crime in the Congo,' Che said, and flew to Africa to meet with the newly elected Tanzanian President, Julius Nyerere, to gain access for his Cuban guerrillas to the Eastern province of the Congo.

WHAT ABOUT DAG HAMMARSKJÖLD?

The United Nations was eight years old when Dag Hammarskjöld accepted his position as Secretary General in 1953. He was a bachelor, leading to rumors that he was gay, to which he stated that he could not have accepted his position at the UN if he were a homosexual because being a homosexual in America was outlawed.

The blue-eyed Swedish diplomat wore crisp gray suits with blue ties, spoke four languages, had a PhD in economics, and was groomed to be a civil servant. In a radio interview with Edward R. Murrow, he said he was influenced by Meister Eckhart and the medieval mystics "for whom self-surrender had been the way to self-realization."

His uptown apartment was filled with art. His social life was rich with music, poetry, philosophy, friendships with artists, conversations with people he encountered in daily life. After his death, in his briefcase, along with Rainer Maria Rilke's *Elegies and Sonnets*, was a copy of *I and Thou* by Martin Buber. He had begun to translate the text into Swedish, "interested in Buber's diagnosis of the political and military problems underpinning the Cold War... problems of trust, communication, and human behavior."[18]

He brought a fresh spirit to the UN as an internationalist and strategist who intervened in Cold War hot spots—Korea, the Suez Canal, Cambodia—to urge diplomacy over use of force, neutrality over supremacy, equanimity over power. He would not automatically side with the big powers or allow the UN to assume a passive role as a conference-based organization. "In our age, the road to holiness necessarily passes through the world of action," he said.

He spent a month traveling through Africa and committed the UN as an ally in the new nation-building efforts. When violence escalated in the Congo after the election of Lumumba, he understood this as a turning point in the creation of a new world order. "It happens to be the Congo; it happens to be now; it happens to be me."

The peace-keeping force he sent to the Congo was too little, too late, and no match for the saboteurs operating in the shadows of international law and order. Heartbroken by Lumumba's murder and his inability to prevent a war, Hammarskjöld decided to advocate for a cease-fire by meeting CIA-backed Mobutu in person. He was warned not to fly into hostile territory, but was determined to handle the peace-keeping mission directly.

Just after midnight on September 18, 1961, Dag Hammarskjöld's plane went down over British-controlled Northern Rhodesia, near the border of the Congo. His security guard, the sole survivor, reported that there had been an explosion on the inside of the plane before it crashed. Then he died unexpectedly in the hospital. Eye-witnesses reported that the plane was hit by gunfire from another plane. The official word was pilot error.

The case is being re-opened based on recent evidence assembled by Susan Williams. She writes that President Kennedy called Stewart Linnér into the oval office the Swedish diplomat Hammarskjold sent to the Congo to uphold the UN Charter. Kennedy apologized to Linnér for putting pressure on Dag to implement U.S. policy in the Congo, which Dag had refused to do. And now it was too late. "I realize now," Kennedy said, "that in comparison to Dag, I am a small man. He was the greatest statesman of our century."[19]

The gesture signaled Kennedy's change of heart toward the region; and nine months later, he was eliminated and the evidence quickly locked up.

AND MALCOLM X?

"You'll never get Mississippi straightened out, not until you start realizing your connection with the Congo."[20] Malcolm X returned from Africa in 1964 and integrated his internal and external maps. He unified the field. When he shifted the focus to global consciousness, Malcolm became a political shaman whose powerful message reached international leaders, college students, people on the streets, anyone open to the reality.

Malcolm went to the UN to attack the U.S. for crimes against humanity. "Instead of going to Congress and the President to appeal to racial justice, you take the U.S, you take the criminal, to court," Manning Marable said in a video interview. "When you do that, you become an enemy of the state."[21]

Malcolm X: "When I **am** dead—I say it that way because from the things I **know**, I do not expect to live long enough to read this book in its finished form—I want you to just watch and see if I'm not right in what I say: that the white man, in his press, is going to identify me with "hate"—and that will help him to escape facing the truth that all I have been doing is holding up a mirror to reflect, to show, the history of unspeakable crimes that his race has committed against my race."[22]

On February 21, 1965, Malcolm X greeted the gathering of the Organization of Afro-American Unity at the Audubon Ballroom on 165th Street in Harlem. A commotion broke out to divert attention, and five men opened fire. "His big body suddenly fell back stiffly, knocking over two chairs; his head struck the stage floor with a thud."[23]

There were twenty-one gunshot wounds to his body. He was thirty-nine years old.

The next day *The New York Times* wrote that Malcolm X was "an extraordinary and twisted man" who "turned many true gifts to evil purpose"[24] and *Time Magazine* called him "an unashamed demagogue" whose "creed was violence."[25]

Ossie Davis delivered the eulogy at the Faith Temple Church of God in Harlem:

"Did you ever talk to Brother Malcolm? Did you ever touch him, or have him smile at you: Did you ever really listen to him? Did he ever do a mean thing? Was he ever himself associated with violence or any public disturbance? For if you did you would know him. And if you knew him you would know why we must honor him: Malcolm was our manhood, our living, black manhood. This was his meaning to his people. And in honoring him, we honor the best in ourselves."

Alex Haley: "He digressed on the dangers he faced. 'But, you know, I'm going to tell you something, brother—the more I keep thinking about this thing, the things that have been happening lately, I'm not all that sure it's the Muslims. I know what they can do, what they can't, and they can't do some of the stuff recently going on… I think I'm going to quit saying it's the Muslims.'

"Then—it seemed to me such an odd, abrupt change of subject. 'You know, I'm glad I've been the first to establish official ties between Afro-Americans and our blood brothers in Africa.' And saying goodbye, he hung up."[26]

A History of Glory and Dignity

Strangely, sadly, a month after I received his email, on April 1, 2011, Manning Marable passed away. Like Malcolm X, he did not live to see the release of his book later that month. *Malcolm X/A Life of Reinvention* was hailed by the establishment—the *New York Times*, Harvard, Princeton, Georgetown—as a defining text.

But black intellectuals and activists came together at a gathering in Harlem, some outraged, to argue the book's weak analysis and strange alignment with a system Malcolm X sought to bring down, that the work was an establishment-funded project completely out of step with what was happening on the streets, that it watered down Malcolm's radical message of self-empowerment, that the attempt to "humanize" Malcolm by focusing on his private life was not history but voyeurism—"a contradictory political reshaping and distortion—a lie really—of the life and times of Malcolm X," wrote publisher and editor Paul Coates, which "demands a strong critical response."[27]

Humanize Malcolm X?

According to Church Committee findings, declassified documents, and extensive historical research, Malcolm X was murdered by agents of the Nation of Islam in collaboration with the FBI and the NYPD.[28]

In 1975 the Church Committee went on record stating that Allen Dulles, head of the CIA at the time, ordered Patrice Lumumba's assassination as "an urgent and prime objective."[29] The State determined that Lumumba was a Communist, and funds to the Congolese leaders who kidnapped, tortured, and assassinated him on January 17, 1961, came directly from the CIA.

Patrice Lumumba was the second African leader assassinated by agents of former colonial masters. Felix Moumie of Cameroon was poisoned in 1960. In 1962 U.S. intelligence helped engineer the arrest and imprisonment, for twenty-seven years, of South African freedom fighter, Nelson Mandela. Sylavanus Olympio, leader of Togo, was killed in 1963; Ben Barka, Moroccan revolutionary theorist and leader, in 1965; Eduardo Mondlane, leader of Mozambique Frelimo, in 1969; Amilcar Cabral, Guinea and Cape Verde, in 1973. Kwanme Nkruhmah of Ghana was ousted in a western-backed coup in 1966.[30]

Patrice Lumumba wrote to his wife four months after independence.

"Dead, living, free, or in prison on orders of the colonialists, it is not I who counts. It is the Congo, it is our people... History will one day have its say, but it will not be the history that Brussels, Paris, Washington, or the UN will teach, but that which they will teach in the countries emancipated from colonialism and its puppets...a history of glory and dignity."[31]

Che Guevara was hunted down and assassinated in Bolivia in 1967 by CIA operatives, who cut off his hands and sent them to Washington as proof that they'd gotten him. But the Bolivian Generals didn't care about the hands of Ernesto Che Guevara, man of the people, the Communist. They went after his diaries.[32]

Dag Hammarskjöld's last diary entry was August 24, 1961.[33]

Is it a new country
In another world of reality?
I awake

To an ordinary morning with gray light
Reflected from the street....
The seasons have changed
And the light
And the weather
And the hour.
But it is the same land.
And I begin to know the map
And to get my bearings.

I Begin to Know the Map
East Africa, 1971

A story has its own logic, how you find it, or it finds you. If I hadn't met Rosemary, I wouldn't be writing this.

Rosie joins the Peace Corps and is placed at a teacher's college on the outskirts of Nairobi. She falls in love with her Kikuyu Peace Corps trainer, Maxwell Kinyanjui, falls in love with Kenya and never looks back.

There we are, bouncing in the back of the lorry through the desert near Ethiopia, our teeth black from desert dust, laughing, Africans laughing too, red teeth from chewing red root, two red-faced women chewing red root with black teeth, laughing.

Laughing with Rosemary makes me whole again. Rosemary, the herb of memory.

Kenya is celebrating *Uhuru*, ten years of freedom from colonial rule. Jomo Kenyatta, Mau Mau freedom fighter, is President. Tribal tensions. World Bank moves in. Masai warriors, spears resting on shoulders, walk into Nairobi to invest in the stock market. Idi Amin stages a coup in Uganda. Guns in Kampala, camping at the source of the Blue Nile. Julius Nyerere, President of Tanzania, is a socialist. The West withdraws support. Chinese Maoists in Zanzibar, black suits, red books, building roads. No roaming the island, official cabs only. U.S. State Department brings artists to Nairobi, cultural exchanges, a front for the CIA, people say. Infusion brings "world music" to the West. Drinking Pimms at the Hotel Nairobi. Africans serve me, the mzungu, the European wandering in circles, the walking dollar bill. This is neo-colonialism. I have the means to travel. Travel is cheap. My camera is stolen. I don't care. I see the struggles. I witness.

Living with Hugh in the highlands, tea and coffee plantations, British-controlled corporations replace Kikuyu farming. People bring cabbages and corn to the market.

Men circle up, drums begin, jumping up and down, laughing, joyful.

Up and down, jumping and drumming, energy and time. Pure. Joy.

Lake Rudolph, four-million-year-old human skull found, people fishing with spears, skin is black almost blue. Crocodile over there, they point. Okay to swim here. Okay, I trust you. I swim. A woman offers to sell me a crocodile head.

Sailing with Sultan to a small island in the Indian Ocean. He cracks open a coconut and we drink coconut milk, me a blip of beige in all the boldness. "Pole, pole," Sultan tells me. *Slow, slow.*

Word sounds, flowing, clicking, valleys, nomads, drummers on sailboats, perfume shops, dirty towns, funky bar playing 45s, playing James Brown.

My world flips over, and I am on the edge of the Rift Valley. Zebras, wildebeest, antelopes, gazelles move across the Serengeti Plains, green from the spring rains, blue sky extending forever. Lionesses at dusk approach zebra herd, finely attuned choreography. Stillness. Movement. Unified. Focused.

Hanging out on the outskirts of my encounters between the wild and the civilized, soaking it in through the senses, smelling something familiar, like home, like I am home.

Uhuru. Freedom.

Our family home, a glimmering green and blue earth floating in deep space. Africa, the Mother of our home, where we humans took form, where our stories were born.

"The story is a living thing," African Elder Malidoma Somé assures me when I consult him about protection. "It is alive. You are here to keep it alive."

The Abyss

In the dream, Philip Partridge is standing on the edge of a cliff. I approach him, and he sees me but doesn't want to talk. He seems troubled, turns away and descends down a steep mountain into a canyon.

I Google "remote-control torture in the '50s" and up pops the MKULTRA project of the 1950s, funded by the Amway Foundation, run by the Robert Gunn family in Michigan, tied to the Nazi Regime in Germany and the Bush dynasty, the new world order, the Project for a New American Century, global domination.

Yes, experiments were conducted on prisoners in the '50s. Philip Partridge could have been the subject of an experiment to monitor his thoughts and torture him by remote control.

The first brain implants were surgically inserted in 1874 in Ohio. Amnesty International's website has links to "remote control torture."

I Google the CIA's website and remote-control torture and feel paranoid because the data is on my own computer. Then I stop. I don't need to fact-check remote-control torture to postulate whether Philip Partridge was writing about real or imagined experience. Torture and assassination are overt, official U.S. policy now. *The New York Times* reports that Tuesday is drone day at the White House. President Obama has a "kill list."[34] There's no due process.

The "eyes and ears" Philip Partridge wrote about are on me now. I willingly pay for the tracking device of a spy system that mines my data and DNA for pattern recognition and location. I read in *Wired* magazine[35] about the NSA headquarters in Utah, five times the size of Capitol Hill, built during the Obama administration. No one seems to know about it.

How gigantic is this, Philip Partridge wondered.

When a senior member of the intelligence community, Edward Snowden, came forward to pull back the curtain on the government's rogue surveillance apparatus, he was deemed an enemy of the state, but he revealed the pattern the way raindrops in sunlight reveal a spider web. How Silicon Valley and the Pentagon are partners, how GeoEye is tracking all movement on earth, how the National Security Agency's PRISM program has been collecting personal data from Microsoft, Yahoo, Google, and Facebook for the past five years to "data mine" the private lives of all Americans, international leaders, anyone with a Gmail address or connected with a Gmail user—which is most of the world's internet population—and how information can appear and disappear through filters and monitoring systems, like George Orwell's "memory hole."

Edward Snowden says his work is not about him, that he wants journalists to get the story out about the extent of the interconnected super-systems—financial, corporate, military—that exist to control and extract resources in order to control the dollar, the story, and the thoughts.

Our high-tech Modern Times are fueled by minerals from the heart of Africa. Cell phones, Facebook, GeoEye, Prism, mass surveillance, Silicon Valley, the weapons trade, the War on Terror, drones—these would not exist without minerals extracted from the Democratic Republic of the Congo.

U.S. Special Operations—AFRICOM—is running shadow operations—one a day—in forty-nine of the fifty-three countries in Africa, a fact which the Pentagon denies.[36] The U.S. is arming and training insurgents in these countries to control the populations in order to control the minerals in order to control the message.

Guardian journalist Luke Harding, at work on the manuscript of his new book, *The Snowden Files: The Inside Story of the World's Most Wanted Man.* "I wrote that Snowden's revelations had damaged U.S. tech companies and their bottom line. Something odd happened," he says. "The paragraph I had just written began to self-delete. The cursor moved rapidly from the left, gobbling the text. I watched my words vanish."[37]

Fire and Water, Stomach and Heart

"I have a high stress occupation," I tell my naturopathic physician in the initial interview. "I'm trying to make a case for something I can't explain."

He understands immediately, examines me, and tells me my system is sluggish. "You are a mover. You need to move."

Dr. Metro was a chemical engineer before he became a naturopathic physician and practitioner of five elements Chinese medicine. I tell him about the dream of the county engineer on the edge of the abyss. "Can I interview you about the engineer, remote control torture, and the American system?"

"Absolutely," he smiles.

Chris Metro: "What compels an engineer by oath—because you take an oath as an engineer—is to uphold the truth of the situation, do the correct calculation or adjustment. You do it for the benefit of humanity. When an engineer criticizes the system or points out the correction needed, most of the time the people who are involved in the system take it personally. They identify themselves with the system. I saw it all the time, all the time.

"Engineers, in Chinese philosophy, have a metal quality—what is exact, measurable, just, refined. Metal stands for highest achievement. That's why it symbolizes Mountain. It's not surprising that an engineer looked for a way to ignite a solution through fire, which is transformative and very specific."

I tell him that the engineer set fire to the school the night after the 4th of July.

"Independence. Oh, that's powerful. The engineer wanted to treat the inequality. Education is transformative. He used fire to break down structure. He's standing on the cliff, which is the mountain and descends into the abyss, the darkness—goes into the shadows to transform the cycle and create movement. People in power don't want that. How do they control that? Through any means possible.

"The people who tried to control him probably drove him to the edge. We're still doing this on many levels. We take peoples' pensions away. Indefinite detention. We kill people with drones. We're a culture that's willing to give up its freedoms because of fear.

"There's a state of possession here—ideologies, inner demons, parasites, depression, anxiety. I see it all the time in the clinic. America is stuck in post-Descartes trauma—mind and body are separate. This is the philosophy guiding the schooling and learning. Dialogue is lost, critical thought. People excite themselves through consumption.

"All disease comes from the heart. We live through materialism. That's a stomach function, a corruption in the way they view and receive the world. In the stomach you put material things, put food in there. You feed the heart with joy, love, laughter. In our culture, we're putting material things into the heart. We've flipped the material and immaterial. The heart can't administer this.

"We are not in a system of endless supply. We need to enter a rejuvenation cycle. Water cycle. Water is a time of peace. Water controls fire. Water is cleansing, creates new growth. Water is the most powerful of the elements, the most humble. You can't stop it."

"The story takes place near the Ohio River," I tell him.

"Ohio—the headwaters of the Ohio River—the flow between slavery and knowledge, a tipping point. I worked on the Delta Queen after college. You travel the river—from New Orleans to Pittsburg and the Upper Mississippi to St. Paul. You saw the different cultures and how they viewed social dynamics, the industry in the Great Lakes states, the struggle. There were great laws in place."

EYE OF THE LAW

*Our minds shape the way things will be because we
act according to our expectations.*
Federico Fellini

HOLY EXPERIMENT

In the early 1600s in England, George Fox imagined a social order guided by the *Inner Light*. No King, no Pope, no Middle Man. We can trust ourselves as human beings if we listen to the Quake, the wee small voice, which has many sounds, generated by the Light within, a harmonic resonance, emerging from the silence. Silence is the organizing principle, faith is the energy. Fox spread the *Good News*, walked all over England when he wasn't in jail, to gather people—to become a Society of Friends, the Quakers—to share the power of listening as a way to integrate outside and inside worlds, to self-organize.

The good news spread.

Quakers developed a clothing style. They refused to remove their tall black hats with big rims and bow to the nobility in passing. They refused to take vows, put on a uniform, fight in wars. For which they were thrown in jail, tortured, and killed.

Elizabeth and Robert Edwards' great-great grandparents heard the *Good News*—her people in Holland, his people in Wales—and they left the Old World for the New World.

From the *Genealogy of the Elizabeth Conard Family*:
"In the latter part of June, 1683, twelve families, numbering all thirty three persons, forced by persecution to act in self-defense, but guided by their religious principal of non- resistance by force, and their policy of flight from oppression, bade farewell to the Rhine, and began their journey to the free and quiet home in the wilds of Pennsylvania."

My Ancestors lived in caves until they built the first dwellings in what became the Germantown settlement, *"with hipped roofs... surrounded by their fruitful orchards, and front-*

ed by their avenue of peach trees." They lived in "peace with the red man, a vivid contrast to the troubled and bloody persecutors of Indians and Friends," referring to the witch-burning Puritans, who hated the Religious Society of Friends guided by the Golden Rule and the Inner Light. "In 1688 the first protest against slavery in the new colonies originated with the German Friends."

My Ancestors purchased their property from the biggest landowner in North America, William Penn, a nobleman who was granted this extensive real estate by the Crown to pay off a family debt. William Penn had become a follower of George Fox, and drew on the teachings of the *Inner Light* to frame his *Holy Experiment*. He drafted a Charter of Liberties to guarantee absolute freedom of worship and ensure fair trial by jury and free elections, with a governing body of commoners (the Assembly) and landowners (the Council).

Penn's innovative document included a new and radical idea: Amendments. The power to change the system. "Governments, like clocks, go with the motion men give them," he wrote in 1693. "Then let us try what love can do to mend a broken world."

He designed Philadelphia, opened free schools—except for Jews and Blacks—bought land from Indians, gave servants fifty acres of their own land, *and* owned and traded slaves.

While Penn was back in England doing business with the Crown, the colonists took their liberties to heart, rewrote the Charter, eliminated the Upper House, strengthened the Assembly, ignored British authority, paid few taxes, fought no war, had no public debt, and prospered.

For several decades prior to the American Revolution, the colonists of Pennsylvania, including my Ancestors from Bucks County, lived cooperatively in an unruly society that became a center for politics, science, and commerce. Penn's *Holy Experiment* was not perfect, but he stood by his dream, and Humanism took root.

By the time the Founding Fathers trotted into the City of Brotherly Love to write the United States Constitution, Philadelphia was a multi-cultural party town—taverns everywhere, co-mingling among the races—and the *Pennsylvania Society for Promoting the Abolition of Slavery* was gaining power, a direct threat to the economic order. So the assembled Fathers designed a document to rein it in, based on the philosophy of Enlightenment—beautiful ideas, elegant language, white male landowners possess the power.

The Founders did, however, include the legacy from the Holy Experiment—the loophole. Amendments. The Quake. Good news.

The Fourteenth Amendment
April 17, 1864

Clear and beautiful.
The girls fixed the flower beds.
Jesse marked out for corn.
Robert has been running around all day,
the Lord knows where, I don't.

Seven months after Elizabeth's notation, Abraham Lincoln won re-election after campaigning to abolish slavery and guarantee equal protection and voting rights to all citizens—what become the Thirteenth, Fourteenth, and Fifteenth Amendments.

Five months later, on April 9, 1865, General Lee surrendered to General Grant at Appomattox Court House, Virginia. Mrs. Goodrich's grandfather, Hannibal Hawk Williams, was one of the soldiers present at the surrender. The Civil War was officially over.

Two days later, on April 11, 1865, Lincoln gave a speech advocating voting rights and literacy for the Freedmen, coupling his vision for equal protection with the mission of equal education. John Wilkes Booth was in the crowd. "That means nigger citizenship," he said to a companion. "That is the last speech he will ever make."[38]

Lincoln's successor, Andrew Johnson, did not hold to the promise of forty acres and a mule for the Freedmen, in reparations for the generations of slave labor. There would be no economic foundation to build a dream on. Instead he returned property seized by the Union Army back to the master class, and a broken American century began.

Three years and three months after Lincoln's last speech, the Fourteenth Amendment was ratified on July 9, 1868. *Equal Protection for all citizens.*

Good News.

SOCIAL ENGINEER
IN CONVERSATION BEGINNING 2003
AND CONTINUING, CINCINNATI

"Nathaniel Jones might help you with the story," Mrs. Goodrich advises. "He is a former Civil Rights leader and later became a federal judge. He lives in Cincinnati."

I Google The Honorable Judge Nathaniel Jones. He worked in U.S. Justice Department in Northern Ohio under Robert Kennedy, was appointed to the Kerner Commission on Civil Unrest by President Johnson, served as General Counsel of the NAACP for a decade during the Nixon years, argued major cases in the Supreme Court, and was named to the federal bench by President Carter.

"I attempted to absorb a disciplined approach to learning so as to master the tools and skills of the legal craft," he wrote in his bio. He had worked as a reporter while he was in law school, a storyteller and man of the law. "Charles Hamilton Houston said it best. A minority lawyer must be a social engineer.'"

Judge Jones joined the firm of Blank Rome as senior counsel after he retired from the federal bench. I enter the highrise in downtown Cincinnati, push the elevator button to the seventeenth floor, never having been in a Cincinnati highrise, or met an NAACP attorney or a federal judge. The elevator is going up, up, and I look down and my boots are scruffy and the elevator door opens.

Judge Jones welcomes me into his office, a handsome, energetic figure, relaxed and alert. He gestures for me to sit opposite him at a large desk with a view of the city on the river. I unpack the tape recorder and look around. Sturdy bookshelf with big legal books. A photograph of the Judge with Nelson Mandela catches my eye. So many stories, so many opinions. I look at the legal warrior, a social engineer, to sense a way to begin.

We begin with the movement, the political muscle behind the NAACP.

Judge Jones: "For a long time Ohio had more NAACP branches, was probably the strongest state conference in the organization. A lot of national attention was focused on Ohio. Location. Interesting state, hybrid state. Northern Ohio, a lot of union activity. Steelworkers union. Michigan was active. Detroit. Pontiac.

"The NAACP was in close collaboration with the union movement during the 1948 Truman campaign. That was my first campaign. It was really exciting. Walter White was the Assistant Secretary of the NAACP, then became top executive, a position he held until his death in the 1950s. He was a very aggressive person, remarkable man, well-connected. Wendell Wilkie, Eleanor Roosevelt, they all looked at Walter White as the guy. He led a delegation to advise Truman about what was happening to the black GI's after they returned. Black GI's were getting beaten and denied jobs.

"Truman was quite upset at what he heard and appointed a commission in 1946 to study the situation and bring him a report. The Commission's recommendations formed the civil rights plank of the Democratic campaign of 1948 that Truman ran on. That's what triggered Strom Thurman and others to walk out of the Democratic convention in 1948 and form the Dixiecrat Party.

"Everyone assumed that the Dixiecrats would take away the traditional Democratic base in the South. However, the Democrats formed a strong coalition in the East and Midwest and far West. And it worked. Truman carried Ohio. Without Ohio, Truman couldn't have won."

It Was For the Cause

Susan: "How would Imogene Curtis, the leader of the school fight in Hillsboro, connect with the NAACP? What was the channel?"

Judge Jones: "It was the Black press. *Cleveland Call and Post. Columbus Call and Post. Pittsburg Currier. Buckeye Review.* Newsletters. Churches. The NAACP branches had a committee structure. Many of the lawyers lending their services were from as far away as Cleveland and Akron. In those days, they weren't in it for the pay. It was for the cause. They took Greyhound buses to Columbus or Dayton and participate in the strategy meetings.

"Dayton had a secretary of the branch, Miley Williamson. She was the liaison between the Dayton and Hillsboro branches. The lawyers would hold day-long meetings and wind up at her house where she provided dinner. Russell Carter and Jim McGee were key Dayton lawyers. Very committed people."

Susan: "One of the Mothers mentioned the name Motley."

Judge Jones: "Constance Baker Motley. She was one of the preeminent civil rights lawyers all through the South. She was a very young lawyer at this time. President Johnson appointed her to the Federal District Court and she later became Chief Judge of the Southern District of New York. The Honorable Judge Motley. She is on senior status now.

"I'll get you her chambers number. I'm sure if you had a conversation with her, her memory would be jogged. She'd remember the Hillsboro case."

READ MY BOOK

The Honorable Constance Baker Motley answers the phone, the woman who defended the marching mothers in federal court, faced off arch segregationists in the South, argued cases before the Supreme Court, became a New York state senator, served as President of the Borough of Manhattan, drew up revitalizations plans for Harlem, and was a mother, grandmother, and priestess of the Law. Her voice is melodious and resonant, with an East Coast accent. She comes from a Connecticut family, rooted in Nevis, an island in the West Indies. Her voice has a lilt.

"What do you want to know?" she asks.

"Do you remember the women of Hillsboro, Ohio?"

"No, I never had the opportunity to personally connect. My role was strictly in the courts. I was on the staff of the NAACP Legal Defense Fund, headed by Thurgood Marshall.

"A local branch would write a letter to the LDF for assistance. The suit was filed in the nearest federal court. The court would give us notice that in sixty days or six months the case would have to come up and we would have to appear. I would have a local attorney, who was admitted to the federal court, who would move my admission for the purposes of the case.

"There were two Ohio lawyers who worked with the NAACP. I remember staying with someone in Dayton who drove me to and fro. She was probably president of the branch.

"The Hillsboro story. It was probably true in a lot of northern communities. But unless blacks opposed segregation, nothing was done."

"What do you think white people are afraid of?" I ask her.

Judge Motley: "Segregation remains deeply embedded in America. We sued the federal government—Washington, D.C.—in those five cases that formed *Brown*. The schools are segregated in many places because the housing is segregated. Unless you have strong agency in the state enforcing these laws, there's not much change."

She talks about real estate practices in New York and the class differences across racial lines. "Employment discrimination is where you find most of the civil rights cases now. I think the problem of the poor is greater than race discrimination. It's poverty today. We seem to make no progress. Not much attention is paid to these problems. There are some efforts being made, but not on the scale that they should be. There is no major effort out there."

"Does anything stand out to you from the Hillsboro case?" I am fishing for some personal details from her memory of those times or town or the people, but she signals that she's done with the conversation.

"Read my book. It's all in there."

I open *Equal Justice Under Law* and re-read Judge Motley's account from 1963, when she went down to Birmingham to reinstate eleven hundred school children who had been expelled during the "children's crusade." She paints a visceral picture of going to the Birmingham jail to work for the release of Dr. King and Reverend Abernathy. She had just returned to New York.

Constance Baker Motley: "I received a telephone call at three a.m. The voice at the other end said, 'This is Robert Smith. They got Medgar.' Medgar (Evers) had been shot by a sniper waiting for him in the bushes at the fork in the road... My life became personally entwined with the life of Medgar. I had spent as much time with him in Jackson as with anyone else in the civil rights movement. I knew he ran a high risk in Mississippi, but when he was cut down, I decided that the price we were paying to end segregation there was too high. The mental anguish was so great that I did not think I would ever get out of bed again. I never returned to Mississippi until 1983. It took thirty years and three trials to convict his killer. Merlie never gave up the pursuit of his killer."[39]

Medgar Evers was a soldier in WWII, but couldn't vote in Mississippi. He dressed as a sharecropper, penetrated plantations looking for Emmet Till's killers in 1955, became Field Secretary for the NAACP in Mississippi, traveled the South, documented abuses, registered voters, spoke out, inspired youth. "You can kill a man," he said, "but you can't kill an idea."

Eye of the Law

Nine months after our conversation, on September 29, 2005, the Honorable Constance Baker Motley passed away at the age of eighty-four. U.S. Congressman from Georgia and civil rights leader, John Lewis, wrote in his press release: "In the heart of the American South, during the early days of the Civil Rights Movement in the late '50s and '60s, there were two lawyers that made white segregationists tremble and gave civil rights workers hope—Constance Baker Motley and Thurgood Marshall. When someone mentioned that one of them was coming to town, we knew there would be a shake-up for the cause of justice."[40]

I open her book again to a random page to see what the good judge has to say, and I hear her deep, full, melodic voice.

Judge Motley: "I had never heard of the *Plessy* case until I went to work for LDF [Legal Defense Fund] in 1945. My constitutional law class at Columbia did not include a discussion of *Plessy* or any other race case. Civil rights law as a major development in twentieth century jurisprudence had not yet begun. I did learn at Columbia, however, that national policy is established as much by a Supreme Court decision on a major constitutional issue as by a law enacted by Congress. After the Supreme Court's decision in *Plessy,* segregation became national policy."

Homer Plessy was told to move to the colored section of the train in Louisiana. But Mr. Plessy did not want Louisiana to tell him where to sit, and his case traveled all the way to the Supreme Court, which agreed with Louisiana.

The 14th Amendment's *equal protection* became *separate but equal.*

Jim Crow. Two societies.

Judge Motley: "Now ask yourselves. Where would African Americans be today if the Supreme Court's 1896 decision in *Plessy* had gone the other way? Now we must ask ourselves: What would twenty-first century America be like?"

One Justice opposed the decision.

Judge Motley: "In Justice Harlan's lone dissent, we find the germination of our twentieth century legal heritage."

Justice John Marshall Harlan from Kentucky: "The white race deems itself to be the dominant race in this country. And so it is, in prestige, in achievements in education, in wealth, and in power."

He affirmed white power, then leveled it by law.

"But in view of the Constitution, in the eye of the law, there is in this country no superior dominant ruling class of citizens. There is no caste here. Our Constitution is color-blind, and neither knows nor tolerates classes among citizens. In respect of civil rights, all citizens are equal before the law. The humblest is the peer of the most powerful."[41]

Outside the Matrix of Justice

What if the marching mothers and their children had been invited into our school and we heard stories about their lives and their protest? What if their memories outside the window had merged with our memories inside the window to create a bigger picture of our community, one with more spiritual and social dimension? What if this memory web had become the foundation for our emotional well-being and our Commonwealth? What would twenty-first century America be like if our memories had infiltrated the barrier? Instead...

Mrs. Goodrich: "Mrs. Curtis used to write letters, and she was not paranoid when she said that some of the letters that she wrote were intercepted right here in Hillsboro. And she would go out of the community to other post offices to mail her letters. I don't know if she was on the FBI list, but she certainly had suspicions and knew that some of her letters were not being mailed. They were intercepted."

People working for the postal service in Hillsboro would have been contacted by federal agents. Folks perusing the morning paper over their percolated cups of Maxwell House and bowls of Cheerios would be reading about Khrushchev and King, but not about the real troublemakers who operated outside the matrix of justice as covert agents of terror for the State, directed by J. Edgar Hoover. That story wasn't out yet, the one about the darkness hanging around town, killjoy of spirits, the cold war penetrating our child bodies and thoughts like an icy draft, dangerous, deadly. We felt it but couldn't name it. No one had words for it. It was covered up by progress.

Who intercepted Imogene's letters? Who bugged Philip Partridge's home? I'm not looking for trouble. Trouble appeared in Hillsboro on its own.

"This is not a fairy tale." Mrs. Goodrich says.

Intercepted

On the night of March 8, 1971, during the Mohammed Ali/Joe Frazier fight at Madison Square Garden, eight anti-war radicals—*The Citizens Commission to Investigate the FBI*—planned and executed a break-in at the FBI storage facility in Media, Pennsylvania. They gambled their futures on the security guards being glued to the TV to watch the fight, cheering crowds masking any sound. Their plan worked and they were never caught.

They stole FBI records and methodically parceled them out to journalists and members of Congress. The documents exposed massive infiltration and domestic surveillance against political activists, black leaders, institutions, community organizers, and universities.

Betty Medsger broke the story for *The Washington Post.*[42] Three months later Daniel Ellsberg released *The Pentagon Papers* that exposed the lies, betrayals of oaths, and crimes against humanity conducted by the past four Presidents from Truman on.

U.S. Attorney General Edward Levi called the covert operations to task and established new FBI guidelines to keep agents within the bounds of the federal law, guidelines that were overturned by Attorney General John Ashcroft in 2002, to unleash "nearly unbridled power to poke into the affairs of anyone in the U.S."[43]

From 1975 to 1976, Congressional hearings led by Idaho Senator Frank Church challenged the FBI and CIA "dirty tricks"—assassinations, training of death squads, engineering of coup d'etats domestically and internationally, all without Congressional approval. *The U.S. Senate Select Committee to Study Governmental Operations with Respect to Intelligence*—the Church Committee—published fourteen reports.

Someone on the committee noticed the name COINTELPRO and insisted on following the clues. COINTELPRO—the FBI's COunter INTElligence PROject—was a shadow operation inside the FBI, active from 1956 to 1971.

Imogene Curtis and Philip Partridge were not paranoid. They were targeted.

Informally, Senator Church called the intelligence agencies "rogue elephants."

Senator Frank Church: "The technological capacity that the intelligence community has given the government could enable it to impose total tyranny, and there would be no way to fight back because the most careful effort to combine together in resistance to the government, no matter how privately it was done, is within the reach of the government to know. Such is the capability of this technology... I know the capacity that is there to make tyranny total in America, and we must see to it that this agency and all agencies that possess this technology operate within the law and under proper supervision so that we never cross over that abyss. That is the abyss from which there is no return."[44]

The social engineers fighting to unify the society through equal protection were shadow-boxing against covert, internalized, systemic racism and a deadly game for geopolitical world domination, a "grand strategy" of complete control of earth's resources through supremacy in the military, marketplace, media, and most of all, memory.

MEMORY ENGINEERS

My brother-in-law, Michael, remembers the billboards going up after the *Brown* decision in his Midland, Texas hometown, same hometown as George W. Bush, different high schools. *Martin Luther King is a Communist! Earl Warren is a Communist!* Texas oil billionaire H.L. Hunt, who had close ties to LBJ, J. Edgar Hoover, and the mob, funded the billboards, and also funded *Lifeline* radio broadcasts that went out to stations in nearly four hundred cities in America, relentlessly attacking Dr. King almost daily.[45]

Book II, Final Report, section D, (Church Committee) Using Covert Action to Disrupt and Discredit Domestic Groups:[46]
"A magazine was asked not to publish favorable articles about him (*Dr. King*). Religious leaders and institutions were contacted to undermine their support of him. Press conference questions were distributed to 'friendly' journalists... FBI agents were being instructed to neutralize Dr. King because he might become a 'messiah' who could 'unify, and electrify, the militant black nationalist movement if he were to 'abandon' his supposed 'obedience' to white liberal doctrines (nonviolence) and embrace black nationalism."

Book II, Final Report, The Black Panther Party:
"One technique used by COINTELPRO involved sending anonymous letters to spouses intended, in the words of one proposal to 'produce ill-feeling and possibly a lasting distrust' between husband and wife, so that 'concern over what to do about it' would distract the target from 'time spent in the plots and plans' of the organization. Priests who allowed their churches to be used for the Black Panther breakfast programs were targeted, and anonymous letters were sent to

their bishops. The Bureau also encouraged 'gang warfare'... would send anonymous letters to 'intensify the degree of animosity between the two groups' and cause 'retaliatory action which could disrupt the BPP or lead to reprisals against its leadership."

Former Black Panther and journalist, Mumia Abu-Jamal, a political prisoner since 1982, writes from prison: "The efforts of the FBI against teachers, professors, workers, socialists, Black nationalists, and others reveal the deep political nature of the agency, the Justice Department, and the United States government as a whole. They were agents neither of order or of law, but of capital. Anyone who merely questioned that arrangement, who thought that society could be organized on a more fair, rational basis, was seen as an enemy; in the words of the FBI itself, 'no holds were barred.'"[47]

The social engineers fighting for equal protection were up against the state's shadow operation designed to divide and conquer.

And the social engineers were winning.

Buzz Word

Judge Jones: "*Brown* did not require de-segregation. All it required was that there be no segregation. The LDF was doing primarily southern cases. The NAACP was doing the northern cases. Bob Carter got the northern trust going. When I got there, that's when we really cranked up and tried some major cases."

Judge Jones was General Counsel of the NAACP from 1968 to 1979.

"We had to prove that segregation was caused by the state authority using its power—restrictive covenants, public housing authorities, and so forth—and this all added up to state action. Which meant you had to dig deeper. We had to dig down beneath the surface and demonstrate how the communities—how school authorities—cooperated. We had to do a lot of research, discovery. We had to raise money. Put teams of researchers in the field. Come up with causation. Once we were able to prove that, we were off and running.

"That's what led to the alarm that swept across the country. In the *Milliken* case, the court reached a crossroads.[48] Segregation was so vast and so pervasive that limiting the remedy to Detroit would not correct the problem. The state of Michigan had the primary responsibility for education, it was made a party to the solution, to the remedy.

"Students had to be reassigned to schools some distance from where they lived. That required a state law that they be transported. There had to be two-way integration. And that's what led to all the resistance. When the Congress, politicians, the courts—realized that using legal principals would result in a massive transformation of public schools, there was a political reaction fed by Nixon and his attorney general, their anti-busing fervor.

"If you recall in the '70s when George Wallace ran for President, he came North and was very popular in Michigan because he was railing against 'pointy-headed judges'—federal judges who were ordering 'busing.' The courts were deemed to be going against the will of the people. Busing became the buzz word. Whenever you wanted to denigrate the whole process, you talked about busing and not the vindication of Constitutional rights. And the public seized upon it.

"So those of us involved in desegregation not only had to fight affirmatively to get orders to desegregate, but we also had to work in the black communities to try to get them to stand firm and not throw in with those who were opposed to the remedy.

"A slogan that a number of blacks began to use was how the blacks got trapped: 'You don't have to sit next to a white child to learn.' It played on race pride. Everybody has pride. Blacks have pride. And you don't have to sit next to a white child to learn. That wasn't the issue. The issue was the system.

"So when you attack a court on the basis of a buzz word called busing, the public appetite is whipped up and translated into political force. So, we had in Congress a whole rash of anti-busing legislation, anti-busing amendments trying to tie the hands of the courts.[49]

"They did not attack *Brown*, did not attack the principal. They attacked the remedy. The simple fact is that a right, as *Brown* articulated it, that is without a remedy, is really no right at all. It becomes illusory.

"That's what was before the Supreme Court in the *Milliken* case."

REMEDY

Just before FBI shadow operations were exposed, and the *New York Times* began to release the *Pentagon Papers*, Michael Kean published his desegregation research, *Hillsboro, Ohio: A Case Study in School Desegregation, The Ohio State University Faculty Research Journal, 1970,* co-authored with his professor and mentor, Dr. Charles Glatt.

Dr. Michael Kean: "Charlie Glatt was a remarkable and committed man. A white southerner from Louisiana, he had never interacted socially with a black man until he served in the Army in the mid-'50s. It was then that he underwent some type of almost existential conversion, and worked in support of the cause of justice the rest of his life. I worked on the Neshoba County, Mississippi desegregation plan with him. That was the location of the film *Mississippi Burning*. His specialty was educational demographics—population trends and shifts. He had the tools of a demographer, and was particularly interested in school districts and urban patterns."

Dr. Glatt was contracted by U.S. District Court Judge Carl Rubin to design a long-term regional integration plan for the Dayton school system, to be completed and implemented by fall, 1976. The school board hired Dr. William (Bill) Gordon, also a renowned desegregation planner in the emerging field that integrated legal and social systems, urban planning, economic systems, education, and community activism.

NAACP attorneys were pressing the district for immediate integration of two elementary schools to "relieve some of the anxiety and anger in the black community...and improve their conception of one-way busing," NAACP attorney Nathaniel Jones was quoted in the Dayton paper.

James McGee, who represented the marching mothers in the '50s, was now the Mayor of Dayton, the first African

American elected to that position. All of the players involved wanted to achieve racial balance, as directed by the courts, without the chaos and violence that marked other cities like Boston and Louisville.

Charlie Glatt wore leisure suits, had a bold relaxed style. He initiated dialogue with teachers, religious leaders, civic and business leaders, parents in the black and white communities—to educate, listen, and respond to the concerns about busing and integration while affirming his personal and professional mission, to equalize educational opportunity.

"The thing we're dealing with is court-ordered change," he told an audience of ministers and teachers. "And believe me, how this community reacts to that change will affect business, industry...everything."[50]

The community reactions were fierce—racists vehemently opposed to integration, black parents angry about one-way desegregation, white parents who didn't want black teachers, black teachers who didn't want the abuse in white schools, people who did not want an outsider getting paid big bucks to tell them what to do. One of the school board members suggested that Dr. Glatt maintain a low profile and let the board take the heat. "He just shrugged and smiled that slow smile and said, 'I have my job to do.'" [51]

He got threatening calls, carried a small pistol in his briefcase, varied his routine, changed cars, and often spent nights away from his hotel, staying in the homes of friends.

"I don't see myself as a savior," he told a reporter for the *Dayton Daily*, "but I do feel an obligation to apply the knowledge I have."[52]

On September 19, 1975, the day the article came out in the *Dayton Daily,* Neal Bradley Young walked into the Old Post Office in downtown Dayton, a federal building that also housed the U.S. District Court. Extra security had been added because of recent bomb and death threats related to court-ordered desegregation, but no guards had been placed near the air-conditioned office of Charlie Glatt. Neal Bradley Young walked into the office, pulled out a handgun and shot Dr. Glatt in the chest and, after he had fallen to the floor, walked over and shot him in the head. Guards heard the shots, saw the man emerge from the office, and seized him, although the man offered no resistance and yielded his gun.

"I did what I had to do," he said, according to one of the guards.

CROSSROADS
MILLIKEN V. BRADLEY, 1974

Judge Jones: "We won it up until the Supreme Court. The Supreme Court reversed five to four. That's when everything came down. It was a lost opportunity for this country, and the Supreme Court failed the test."

Justice Potter Stuart was the deciding vote, the judge on the Sixth Circuit Court of Appeals who wrote the majority opinion in *Clemons v. Board of Education of Hillsboro*. The federal courthouse in downtown Cincinnati is named after him. He voted against *Milliken*.

"Why? Why did Potter Stuart betray the cause? He knew the forces at play."

Judge Jones: "White superiority and black inferiority. When the rubber hits the road, there is a belief that whites should not be penalized to accommodate blacks. Although the Detroit plan was not designed yet, it would have assigned some of the suburban white kids to inner city black schools. It wouldn't be fair to 'punish' suburban people by asking them to participate in the Detroit remedy. That's when Potter Stuart got off the bus."

Judge Jones writes in his book, *Answering the Call*, "Given that the decision in the *Milliken* case was five to four, had Justice Stewart urged his Supreme Court colleagues to remand, it is possible that we would have broken the back of urban school segregation."[53]

"*Milliken* demonstrated the pervasiveness of racial discrimination throughout all of America's institutions, whether they were in the North or South. If the decision had gone the other way, the educational landscape of the country would be totally different."

"How would it look?"

Judge Jones: "If it was possible for the problems of education to be approached on a regional basis, there would be no hiding place. When children are thrown together into common schools, the climate changes, there's a change in culture. Without that, children remain isolated.

"The Detroit schools right now, it's catastrophic. We are returning to the culture of *Plessey*—to state's rights, to privatizing schools, vouchers."

Susan: "I ask the women in Hillsboro, 'So the school's been integrated since 1956, is the community integrated?' They say, 'No, it's not. It's still a very segregated community.' It seems like no matter what the courts decide, if the community is still segregated, how can you have real transformation in society?"

Judge Jones: "Why is the community still racially isolated? Because the other patterns haven't been altered. To affect social change, you must operate on all levels. Desegregation of schools is one strategy, but you've got to have other strategies at work. Apparently, Hillsboro has not had the kind of leadership that has attacked the problem on a broader scale."

EDUCATION LANDSCAPE
HILLSBORO, 2012

David Ornette Cherry and I are performing for the Hillsboro Middle School. Louise Steinman introduced us after I performed *No Strangers Here Today* in her ALOUD series at the Central Library in Los Angeles. She commissioned a collaboration with David for a repeat performance in 2007, which changed everything.

No Strangers Here Today is a movement monologue with live keyboards and electronic soundtrack, the epic story of the Abolitionist Movement, with Elizabeth Edwards' diary entries as the heartbeat and David's haunting sound score as the emotional bed. When David opened the diary to see Elizabeth's handwriting, he began to weep. We both did.

Friendship. Hard to do, life-changing, on-going integration. David created the soundtrack for the theatrical version of *The Hillsboro Story,* which ends with the final scene in Part II, "Friendship." He loves the piece. "Just write *The End*," he says. He was in Hillsboro getting the town vibe and talked his way into the old high school just before it was torn down. He created and recorded the haunting piano solo, "Friendship," in the old auditorium. Memory music.

I went to visit his Watts, LA neighborhood, where his music was born—on the streets, in garage bands, in schools, in marching bands, along Central Avenue, where his parents became part of the avant-garde of free jazz and poetry, where his *Organic Nation Listening Club*[54] took root. My Muse kicks up a lot of dust. "*Friendship*. It's perfect. Just write *The End*."

But the story isn't over, I always say.

This is the second time we are performing both shows in Hillsboro. Both shows were piloted in the town to test the reception with the real people. Affirmative! The first time David and I performed *No Strangers* at Southern State Community College, we came out for a Q&A after the show. A tiny, elderly woman in the front row immediately raised her hand. "I bought a Buick from your Dad," she proclaimed. A middle school student raised his hand. "Why aren't we taught about this?" he asked.

All of the schools—Lincoln, Webster, Washington, Hillsboro High School—have been torn down. This brand new consolidated complex on a hill on the outskirts of town, has a neo-colonial Nike Town style, with grand entrance, big screens, electronic devices in every room, playing fields, big gym, band room. But no dance space, no black box theatre, no jazz, no magic. Students have to drive or have parents drop them off or take the bus. There are no sidewalks, no bike trails. No one walks to school.

The art of teaching and learning has been replaced by federally mandated standards, the *Common Core*, delivered through Microsoft.[55] Obama's *Race to the Top* is outpacing Bush's *No Child Left Behind,* with more intense corporate "benchmarks." Teachers get good test results or out the door they go, the librarian, Lynn Musser, tells me. She wrote the Ohio library grant that funded our performance. She doesn't have much hope for curiosity. Library budgets are being cut. She's leaving next year. Our show is sandwiched between a beauty college presentation the day before and military recruiters the day after.

David and I are onstage in the cafetorium, preparing to begin the show—noisy, stinky, dishes clattering in the kitchen, a few basic lights on a wide, shallow stage, a sea of faces going way back into space, a fidgeting wave-like motion, teachers stoically standing around with arms folded. I sense that no one gives a damn about the Underground Railroad, and I don't think my mic is working. I look over and there's

David all aglow, sitting at the grand piano in his African garb, surrounded by his African instruments, ready to strike the first note, deep in the dream, ready to take this journey with me.

We begin with the sound of a bell, then a piano solo, then movement, then the stories unfold in a landscape of images. How fugitives from slavery traveled on a network that grew from hundreds of slave uprisings and individual escapes, from the first Society for the Abolition of Slavery in Philadelphia, from free Black settlements, Quaker philosophy, collaborations and communication channels that grew into a powerful human rights movement. How Ripley, thirty miles south of the school was a stronghold of abolitionists. The memories of riding with my grandparents to see the home of the Reverend John Rankin, who left a lantern in his window on a bluff overlooking the Ohio River, to signal fugitives up and down river that this was a safe house. How Eliza in *Uncle Tom's Cabin* was a real woman the Rankins had assisted.[56] How her first escape, in 1837-- when my great-great Grandparents were traveling to Ohio to settle--was followed by her return to engineer the escape of her children and grandchildren from a Kentucky slave owner. How Harriet Beecher Stowe's novel, published in 1852--when Robert Edwards built the red brick safe house ten miles from the school--outsold every other book published in America until then, except the Bible. How Harriet Tubman, in response to an invitation to see a staged production of *Uncle Tom's Cabin* said, "I haint got no heart to go and see the sufferings of my people played out on the stage. I've seen de real ting. And I don't want to see it on no stage or in no teater."[57] How a Kentucky slave trader could make more money kidnapping a free Black, breaking up a family, to force march his "property" to markets in the south, than he could raising tobacco. How a Quaker farmwoman, ten miles from the school, went about the days, tending to life, noting the absence of Strangers on the farm.

David's soundtrack evoked the energy and rhythms of the places and people, the powerful Ohio conductor, John P. Parker, who bought his freedom, patented inventions, operated a bi-racial foundry in Ripley, and risked his life and freedom to bring people across the river and send them up through Brown and Highland Counties.

American history in the landscapes outside the school window.

After the show, the first hand shoots up, a boy staring at David. "Where did you get your shirt?" he asks. I can see the principal is ready to pounce, but David jumps in. "Good question," he says. "It's from Ghana. Do you know where that is?"

Then the story opens up, and we are (not all) poised to take a peek at the global enterprise of history through the music of the story. The students can tell we are gamers. Next question. "Are you two married?" The principal checks his watch.

"Good question," I say. "No, we're collaborators. It's kind of like being married…"

I know they want to know about the real taboo topic in the cafetorium, and I pause… searching for the words to talk about creating… a new language…what that's like… what they think… do they have those experiences… but I don't quite get there… to the core of the question.

The principle seizes the pause, thanks us, and sends everyone on to the next class.

Two young men with long hair stay behind. They want to talk to David, find out more about him, about the music, look at the instruments. They want to do their own music. "It was sad," David said. "The principal came over and called them troublemakers. They were reaching."

David at Bill Fling's Farm, Highland County, 2012

POWER

Judge Jones argued the *Milliken* case before the Supreme Court on behalf of Detroit, holding the state of Michigan responsible for regional school integration, and lost the argument to five men in black robes who turned their backs on Detroit and the vision of full integration in America, turned their backs on children.

Then the justices used the Fourteenth Amendment to grant "equal protection" to corporations.

"They act like a bunch of drunken sailors," Judge Jones says.

Imagine twenty-first century America if Judge Jones sat on the Supreme Court where Clarence Thomas sits snoozing away on his padded bench. "Power, not reason, is the new currency," Thurgood Marshall said when he retired from his well-worn bench.

Judge Jones: "In 1980 Reagan stated that the time had come to remove 'activist' judges from the bench.[58] And that process started and that's been reflected in the make-up of the Supreme Court and you see it now in the make-up of many of the Courts of Appeals."

"Have far to the right will the courts go?"

Judge Jones: "Well, it will go as far as the public allows it to go. Look at the Patriot Act. Basic Constitutional rights are being compromised. Fourth Amendment rights. Search and Seizure. People are just prepared to give up some of their basic rights, all in the cause of national security. The courts are backing off the enforcement of civil rights. We're losing balance. If you're not vigilant, you're going to be like the person who had his throat cut and didn't know until he shook his head. People are totally oblivious to..."

"History?"

Judge Jones: "Ann Richards or Molly Ivins said, when you go to a dance, you dance with the one who brung you. And a lot of people are at the dance now and they forgot who got them there. They're totally oblivious."

"Do you still have faith in the law as an agent of social change?"

Judge Jones: "Oh I do, sure, you can't give up on that. You have to just persist, meet the issue on different levels. Whether it's a racially dominant society or a society dominated by one race over another race, it's a matter of power. Power has a tendency to corrupt and dominate. The challenge is to be able to push back against those who engage in abuse of their power, irrespective of who they are and where they are."

"What took you to South Africa?"

Judge Jones: "I had been working with a team of anti-apartheid lawyers as an election observer. I was with the team way up north in an isolated location. We gathered in the hotel around a TV to watch the ceremony. The votes were in. There were twenty-eight parties that were running for control of the government. The AMC was the strongest, led by Nelson Mandela. It was at midnight when the nation observed a change in government—lowering of the old Nationalist apartheid flag, and the raising of the new flag of South Africa. It was a gripping moment.

"What was it like to meet Nelson Mandela?"

Judge Jones: "Amazing. My wife and I had dinner with him. He was a great listener. Very curious. I was complimenting him on the provision in their constitution that prohibits the death penalty. He felt very strongly about that. We didn't talk about his imprisonment. He was curious how the courts were working in the United States."

Susan: "Given what is going on in Ohio—police shootings, gentrification of black neighborhoods, high school drop-out rates up, drug epidemics, manipulation at the polls, do you think Governor John Kasich has read the *Kerner Report?*"

Judge Jones: "I'm sure he hasn't. But the insights remain relevant."

In 1967 President Johnson appointed Nathaniel Jones—working in Northern Ohio for the Justice Department under Robert Kennedy—to serve as deputy general counsel on the Kerner Commission, the *National Advisory Commission on Civil Disorders.* Riots were breaking out across the country. Watts was only the beginning.

Judge Jones: "The mission proved sobering and urgent, but it afforded the opportunity to participate in a significant historical drama—to drill down deeply into the piles of 'social dynamite' stored up in American cities, and to do so at the command of the president of the United States."[59]

Johnson chose loyal moderates from both parties and expected a document that would appease both during the domestic tensions and escalation of the Vietnam War, a holding pattern while he consolidated his power. But something else happened.

The commissioners and their teams went into the ghettos and witnessed first-hand the betrayal: "White society is deeply implicated in the ghetto. White institutions created it, white institutions maintain it, and white society condones it."[60] The *Kerner Report* uncovered the truth about what was causing "civil unrest" and named the enemy—*pervasive discrimination and segregation in employment, education, housing, the courts, health care.* The report called for massive investment from the federal government toward jobs, education, economic infrastructure, housing, health. But there was Vietnam.

Judge Jones: "It took effort to persuade Dr. Martin Luther King, who was one of our final witnesses, to testify at the commission hearing... King addressed what he deemed to be the overriding issues of poverty, hunger, and the Vietnam War."[61]

"I knew that America would never invest the necessary funds or energies in rehabilitation of its poor so long as adventures like Vietnam continued to draw men and skills and money like some demonic, destructive suction tube," Dr. King said in his 1967 speech at Riverside Church in New York City.

The *Kerner Report* came out on March 3, 1968 and sold a million copies right away. Dr. King's Poor People's Campaign received a much-needed boost from the report,[62] although Johnson turned his back and wouldn't sign it. A month later, on April 4, Dr. King was assassinated. Nixon's law and order campaign, an extension of the Southern Strategy, gained footing. A Democratic Congress passed important legislation in housing, health care, desegregation of courts, job discrimination, but the mission of *Kerner* faded into the background with the election of Reagan and the Democratic Party's shift into neo-liberal economics, endless war, a booming prison-industrial complex, and the new hip segregation—gentrification.

CHILLS

I am selling the family home in Portland, preparing for the next chapter. The realtor shows up with a woman who is moving from Manhattan with her husband, a record producer. She loves the house, says she's getting chills. I'm waiting in the kitchen while she goes through the place, and she comes in and asks me about the civil rights stuff in my office. I tell her about the Hillsboro story. She says, 'My father wrote the Civil Rights Act and Voting Rights Act with Bobby Kennedy.' "

"Wow." I'm staring.

"He was Assistant Attorney General under Robert Kennedy. Then he was the Attorney General."

"Of the United States?"

"Under Johnson," she says, "Nicholas Katzenbach. He's the man in the picture facing off George Wallace. The Kennedys sent him to the South. He was their Justice man down there. He died two years ago. I miss him. He was a great man and father."

"What did he say about what's going on now?"

"He said, 'We did the best we could.' We had to leave town after Nixon came in. Look his obituary up in the *New York Times*."

The obituary described a courageous and eloquent spokesman for the law, an elegant thinker who took personal risks. He faced off arch segregationists in the South and opposed Hoover's wiretapping of Dr. King. And he was integral to two major cover-ups—the *Warren Report,* the investigation of the Kennedy assassination that was locked up immediately, and the *Gulf of Tonkin Resolution* that was LBJ's justification for the invasion of Vietnam.

Later Katzenbach went to Vietnam to witness the war, and became determined to bring the war to a peaceful end.

Too late. Two million Vietnamese lives were lost, fifty-eight thousand American soldiers died fighting, and later another fifty-eight thousand killed themselves. Agent Orange would show up in the offspring. The bombing of Cambodia and the Killing Fields followed. Millions of people like us, going about their days, raising their children, growing food, listening to the stories of the elders. Gone.

She didn't buy the house. I wondered about tracking her down for an interview, but why? She was grieving. Her father was alive in her heart, not in the halls of power.

"I knew Nick," Judge Jones says when I ask him about Nicholas Katzenbach. "The last time I saw him he was stooped over."

HISTORIES ARE NEVER TOLD IN ISOLATION

These places live inside us, in our bodies, and beyond us, in the cosmos.

I jot this down on a little pad I keep beside the driver's seat. I have just taught a *movement and monologue* workshop and asked the group to move through their childhood landscape—to create movement from the memory of the contours, weather, details, trees, wind, textures, shapes. The landscape dances take the stories to a deeper level. I'm not sure how...body cosmology.

I tear the note out of the notepad, an impulse, stuff it in my pocket, and go to meet my son, Quincy, for breakfast, the child formerly known as Jack. There he is, driving up in his black car with the shiny rims, all handsome and ready for action.

"I recognized you from the rims," I tell him after we hug. "Good," he says. "it's working." I laugh. I tell him I'm looking for a signature gesture too—to end the book. He laughs and we head toward the Tin Shed, one of his favorite breakfast spots.

He's leaving soon for the Old Country to connect with his Hungarian roots and make art along the journey, guided by "the healers, not the dealers," his lyrics say. He has just returned from a Ceremony. "The Sun Dance was suppressed," he says. "It's powerful and it works."

I'm thinking about the Shadow Dance. The Spirit Dance.

"When the nights get cold, shadows reaching for your soul, we will be that lighthouse, lighthouse, lighthouse ... help you find your way home."[63] The lyrics from his latest CD, *Remedy*, speak to the spark that will unite us and lead us home.

My child, all children, carry the magic and love of the Ancestors in their memory cells. The power of storytelling—to teach ourselves and our children to remember who we are, how we are responsible for memory, this is the gift we offer for this life, to keep the spirit moving toward the lighthouse of memory, without fear, with trust, to dance with the shadows because we all have them, the demons, who are part of the story too. We move. Quake. Listen. Connect.

Later, after our goodbye hug, I pull the note out of my pocket. I always want more time with my son. Our lives are so swift, like a flash of lightening. Love comes with longing.

On the back of the note I had scribbled these words:

"Histories are never told in isolation." Angela Davis

HEART OF JUSTICE

I imagine a theatre piece with Judge Jones as the jazzy legal storyteller, backed by a saxophone player who underscores the words in a medley, like John Coltrane's *Giant Steps* or *Lonnie's Lament,* words and notes precise, bold, affirming, soulful, everyone in shades of blue, choreographed with moveable furniture, the detective shifting the action and point of view.

I'm writing and imaging the theatre of the story, then have a dream about the saxophone player I am imagining. In the dream, we are collaborating and I am standing next to him, watching him conduct the jazz ensemble. He is earnest and stays focused and wants me to see who is getting down to business. He points to an older guy, a funky horn player on the end of the row, who can really play the music. He wants me to hear the *sound* of it. I stretch my ears to hear more and can't contain my joy. "That's why I love you," I proclaim to the saxophone player, who keeps conducting as he looks over and smiles. I wake up.

Later, I text the real saxophone player *happy holidays* and sign my full name because he might not remember who I am. He texts back *happy holidays.* I text back, *I had a dream about you.* He texts back, *Hope it was a good one.* I text him the dream, in full. *I think it's a good one. What do you think?* He texts back, *That's a good dream. Let's do it.*

Then there's the real encounter that becomes a negotiation, like music, in off-beats.

Here we go again. Again? *Where's your video?* Video?

If you stop at a single school district, Judge Jones argued, the shadow can hide out. Full integration is regional. You have to step out of your comfort zone and get feedback, lots of feedback. Then adjust, stay alert in case you're doing more than you need to. Check your breathing, good deep breath, go into the bones and feel the solid, flexible structure of your body, notice gut reaction because intelligence is rooted down there.

You never have to be ashamed of who you are. The musician's words are new music, a healing sound. He doesn't say yes, and he doesn't say no. He says, *It's your choice.*

I soften my focus and see this other person, who seems edgy. I have no idea why or what to say next. That's the Dance for Democracy. I'm in it, but I can't control it.

Webster Elementary School integrated, but we never did, We-the-Children, straddling the rickety structures of two worlds and expected to land on both feet, upbeat and ready to go. Who was protecting us? Mrs. Mallory was a beautiful role model, and my classmates mostly tried their best; but I don't remember anyone ever talking to me about belonging.

The marching mothers were out on Walnut Street to lift the burden of inequality from my hometown. They weren't troublemakers. They were peacemakers. Even a child of eight understands peace, is uplifted by looking into the eye of the law to see the spirit of love.

PART IV
BELOVED
KALEIDOSCOPE
COMMUNITY

Main Street apartment, 2007, Hillsboro

All art is autobiographical.
The pearl is the oyster's autobiography.
Federico Fellini

BLUE IN GREEN

People in the story—did I come to them or did they come to me?

I struggle with power and freedom. My family and my society marked me. "This side of the grave you will not escape from the marks it has given you," George Orwell says.

No escape from the sad lusty now and then history.

The voices in this story testify to their historical moment on this patch of earth, everyone filling the geography with color and character, everyone a teacher, every story a teaching. We don't know where the conversation is heading. Integration can be mandated, but truly, it's an inside job.

I strategize, fall in love with the mystery, acting and knowing I'm acting, trying to relax, trying to say something about time and choreography, trying to learn to trust life, not fear it, seeking the source, moving toward the borderland where we all belong, where there is no pyramid scheme, no middleman, and history is about how our spirits travel and touch.

A Great Mystery

"Your skin color is deceptive," African scholar and healer, Malidoma Somé told me, looking straight into my heart. So where do I belong?

"We're all Appalachians," John Bryant says. "We're connected by the land."

John was one of the first African American college basketball players at the University of Cincinnati in the '50s, one of four African American teachers hired for the first time in the Hamilton County School District, and the first African American to be hired for the coaching staff at UC as the assistant basketball coach. "I was sitting at the banquet where they were announcing this—that I would be the assistant basketball coach—and Oscar Robinson motioned for me to come over to his table and sit down. He whispered, 'John, the servers from the kitchen said Martin Luther King has just been shot.'"

John is my ally. I took his genealogy workshop at a Quaker conference and resonated with his study of family history, migration patterns, human movement, cultural expression. He saw and promoted both theatre works, has served as chair of the Ohio Humanities for a time and is on the board of the National Underground Railroad Freedom Center, advocating for an "Ohio Room" that pulls together African American and Quaker history, scholarship, poetry, and landscape into stories located in three Ohio memory places—Chillicothe, Oberlin, and Cincinnati. The room hasn't happened yet, but John has a Langston Hughes saga about it.

John and I walk through downtown Cincinnati, and he points to street corners and alleys where an African American church stood, the street where a wagon carrying fugitives passed by, hiding in the back, heading to the outskirts of hate, moving toward freedom.

"How would you show this?' John wonders. Public art, true story.

Fountain Square, which used to be the center of the elegant downtown, is drowned out by giant TV screens broadcasting sports events. Who cares about history? The beautiful old plaza is dwarfed by the U.S. Bank skyscraper surrounded by sports pubs. What would cut through the clutter?

I wander on my own, checking out the elegant neo-classic Netherland Hilton Hotel off Fountain Square, passing through the sky bridge from the hotel mezzanine to the shopping areas. I notice a line along the wall, which does not appear decorative, so what is it? I follow the line past shops through the sky bridge over to the other side, where it ends. At the end is written,

Where is the horizon line? – Yoko Ono

Yoko Ono cut through the clutter. She took me to the edge—between the earth and sky, body and spirit, to a navigational anchor, a way to integrate one part of existence with another.

My brother, John, and I climb to the top of the Appalachian Plateau that looks down into the foothills. The little city of Hillsboro, Ohio sits atop seven hills, like Rome, out there over the horizon line.

I left the town, but the town never left me. Spirits tagged along, swept in by the wind and leaves, looking through windows into other worlds.

There we are, the children heading for school, coming from our different places to meet each other at Webster School and learn and grow and play.

I stretch for truth along the Appalachian highways because it makes me feel better. I don't even know who is driving the Buick anymore. Years pass. Family dramas, divorce, my young son grows into a man. I dream I am driving and there is no steering wheel and I miraculously end up at a revival meeting in a blue tent.

My Chinese medicine doctor says integration is not an ethical issue, from a healing perspective. Integrity is about harmonizing the systems, like jazz. Aligning the energies. The story moves through it all, revealing more of itself, reframing itself, squaring the circle, a fractal in a myriad of stories in time.

I return to the Great Serpent Mound, as I do on every trip to Ohio—the largest earthwork effigy in North America, sited on a bluff above Ohio Brush Creek, where the land was forced up three hundred and fifty million years ago when a meteor hit the earth and made a five-mile wide crater in the sea bed, twenty miles from my house on Danville Pike.

The Serpent is a quarter mile long with seven undulating coils, a spiral tail spinning counter-clockwise, and an open mouth swallowing (or expelling) an egg (or turtle)—the story of the Serpent continues to unfold. LiDar photography penetrates the earth, and archeologists and astronomers confirm what Native Americans have held in their memory field for eons, the story of a cosmic dance embedded in the structure of the earthwork, created five thousand years ago, a remarkable feat of astronomy, geometry, and energy. Who were they? A great mystery.

It's late and I'm alone with the Serpent. The park closes at nine-thirty p.m. I have come to see the summer solstice alignment—two days off—June 23, 2016—but, cosmically speaking, close enough. The sun appears to be going down over the spiral tail. But then I follow the seven coils around the contours of earthwork to the head of the Serpent. Sure enough, the sun is setting in perfect alignment with the egg.

I lie down on the body of the Great Serpent and feel the energy generously nurturing my body. I look out from this place into a darkening sky, filling up with stars and worlds and feel this gift of life, this memory place, this spirit, this *manitou*, reminding me again of the vastness of stories and to please, receive my blessings.

Aligned, I return to the parking lot, climb into the rental car, and head to Hillsboro to find the end of the story.

Watershed Moment

I pull into Pam's driveway like I always do when I stay in Hillsboro. I always stay with Pam. I tried to stay in a motel once to give Pam more space, but it looked like drug deals were going down and the whole motel complex smelled like cigarette smoke and cleaning supplies and old carpeting. "This is not working," I finally called to tell Pam. It was late. She drove down in her PJ's to pick me up. She has been my anchor through it all.

"The Democrats want me to run for Mayor," she calls me in 2014. "Should I do it?"

"Yes!" I proclaim. "It will be an adventure." Plus this could be the end of the book, since I can't seem to find the end. My childhood friend is now Mayor of the town. Perfect!

Pam's opponent is Drew Hastings, the current Mayor. Professional comedian. Republican. Official Jackass. He fired the Fire Department because they were union. He was on the Jay Leno show. "There are more corn rows in the NFL than I have on my farm," he quips to Jay, who brought him on the show as a newly elected small-town mayor of America. He fell in love with the town passing through, bought a farm, and look, now he's the mayor! The joke is kind of funny, if you think about a guy who uses hair products as a farmer, but that's only part of the joke.

"Hillsboro is not a joke," Eleanor says.

I contacted Drew for an interview in the Fall of 2011. He'd been talking to a Hollywood producer about a reality TV show starring him, the mayor. He must have thought I was someone else, because the secretary said that he'd left three hours open for the interview. Three hours? He bought Bells Opera House, got some grant money to fix the roof. Maybe we can go over there and talk about theatre. "The Hillsboro Story" at Bells Opera! But we didn't get to the theatre. The theatre spirits are still waiting for some action because the mayor cut the interview short. He didn't want to talk about economic development or Rick Santorum, who was campaigning for President in Wilmington on an anti-abortion platform. Gotta run, he says, and reschedules for Friday to finish up, and I show up, but he's not there.

Betty Bishop, veteran politician, former mayor of Hillsboro for fifteen years, is Pam's campaign manager. I'm in town for the kick-off. Betty wants to run a positive campaign, and Pam seems ready and willing. "I'm probably crazy," she says. "I don't know what I'm doing." "Yes you do." She has a business head, worked in big organizations, politics, is well-informed, has good people skills, "a common-sense candidate, dedicated to the people of the community," her campaign postcard says. Pam glows. She's always been shy. She shines.

We talk about a regional five-county economic plan, connecting to Sherrod Brown, the Ohio Senator who is spearheading worker-owned manufacturing revivals in northern Ohio. Why can't Hillsboro be a new model for sustainable economics? The farm land is rich, aquifers abound; the perfect place for an energy grid that uses wind, solar, and geothermal. The three community colleges in the region could network with school districts to offer engineering, building, designing, welding, tool and die making, organic food growing—the tools to build a new society and attract young people who have the vitality and want to focus their genius on something other than a low wage jobs or a being cogs in a failing system.

"Win or lose, you can use this as a platform," I say.

Pam was moved by the story of the marching mothers. "I probably wouldn't be doing this if it hadn't been for you coming here and doing that story. I've learned so much and am honored that Elsie showed up at the kick-off event," she says. "That's really big. Win or lose, I feel blessed."

Prosperity. How do you create it? Our parents had dreams. Dad was a Democrat and Charlie was a Republican, but that didn't matter. They brought Rotary Forms Press to Hillsboro from Detroit and helped create jobs for people for decades.

But this is another moment, a watershed moment. The ice caps are melting. Detroit filed for bankruptcy.

I give Pam *The Next American Revolution* by Grace Lee Boggs,[64] the ninety-eight-year-old philosopher and Detroit activist who, with her husband, African American auto worker, Jimmy Boggs, forged a movement from the industrial ruins that is blossoming into urban gardens, humane educational centers.

Grace Lee Boggs:[65]

"We are at a very critical time in the history of the world.... We have to begin re-creating our relationship with one another and with the rest of the world. This is the time to grow our souls. What does it mean to be a human being at this time on the clock of the world? We have to speak to that. We have to create a new American Dream. We have to see that the jobs that paid us income also turned us into consumers and robbed us of some of our creativity and robbed us also of our obligations to one another and robbed us of our relationships to community, and that we have to restore those. We have to begin looking at our children and our educational system in terms of how children can become a part of the solving of our city's problems, and not isolated in classrooms to be given information that they regurgitate so that they can get jobs which don't exist."

Pam campaigns for a year—speaks to high school students, goes door to door, runs a positive, upbeat campaign, sees the cracked sidewalks and struggling families. The Ohio Democratic party taps her for their Main Street Initiative, a bipartisan mayoral network. Rory Ryan, editor of the Highland County Press, enthusiastically endorses Pam and keeps track of the mayor's abuses of power.

Gary Abernathy, the editor of the pro-Drew paper, calls Pam the "kinder gentler" candidate, a homegrown girl, not mayor material. Drew and followers call her challenges to his accountability a "witch hunt."

"Misogyny," I say. "It's deep."

I arrive to help her at the end of the campaign, October, 2015. I want to be there for the victory. We're channeling Dad and Charlie, sitting around talking politics and money, cracking each other up, except instead of lawn chairs with bottles of Schlitz beer, we're on deck chairs with glasses of Chianti, and she's telling me campaign stories.

A police officer approaches her while she is campaigning, slows down the car and drives up next to her. She thinks, "Uh oh, what did I do?" He rolls the window down and gestures for her to come over. "I'm voting for you," he whispers.

County Fair

P: The county fair about did me in. I had to sit in that booth for a week. They were selling confederate flags out there.

S: Whoa.

P: The Democratic booth was on one side and the Tea Party booth was on the other. Yes, the Highland County Tea Party. They had this little game set up. It was about history and if you all the answers right, you got a prize—and I did.

S: What was your prize?

P: I got a hand grenade.

S: A hand grenade?

P: And I took it back to Jim Rooney and he said, 'Oh, I'm going to go win one,' and he came back and said, 'They're all out.' And I said, 'Here, take mine.'

S: We are in serious trouble.

P: So the woman who is a member of the Tea Party in Highland County is running for office. And she'd come over and visit and she said, 'I need to talk to you.' And she sat down and said, 'Two things. Do you know about local currency? You have to look into it. You have to start a local currency.' And I said, 'Why?" And she said, 'When it all goes down, there's not going to be any money. But if we have a local currency, that will help.' So I did a little reading about it.

S: What did you find out?

P: I can honestly say, I can't remember.

S: I understand... But I do believe in small banks, regional banks. My great-grandfather, with six other men, started the White Oak Valley bank in Mowrystown, and they loaned and operated within the region until the 'bank holiday' that closed all the banks. That was local currency. Maybe the Tea Party lady is right

P: And then—second—she said I know somebody who knows somebody in the CIA. She said, 'Did you know that the CIA has looked all over the United States and determined that the safest place to be when it all blows up is Highland County.' And I said, 'Really? That's great!'

S: Why?

P: She said, 'Oh, they're moving in.'

S: Who's moving in?

P: The CIA.

S;   To Highland County?

P: They could be your new neighbor. Weather wise—you know, we've been very lucky with weather, no floods, no tornedos. There's been enough rain. There hasn't been a drought.

S: I think the Tea Party lady is on to something....

P: I said, 'Barb, that's really interesting.' She's the one who brought to light that they are building a million-dollar weight room out at the high school.

S: A million-dollar weight room at Hillsboro High School?

P: Yes. You just have to go day-to-day around here. People have lost touch with reality.

CONCESSION STAND

I tell Pam I will do anything she wants to help with the campaign and she asks me to sell concessions at the football game, Betty's idea. "Sure!" I say. Sell a few hot dogs and bags of popcorn. Watch the game like the old days when I was a cheerleader for the Indians. "I don't suppose anyone is having the mascot discussion around here," I say. She looks at me like I've lost it.

There we are, Lucy and Ethel at the concession stand, where for three solid hours, we scramble to keep up with the long lines and long orders for things I have never heard of—candy with new names—Goo Goo Clusters, Air Heads, Fruit Gusher, Gobstopper, Aba Zabba—and every color of Gatorade you can imagine—turquoise, pink, yellow, green—and nachos with cheese and sloppy joe nachos with or without cheese and deep-fried Oreos, yes cookies that are deep fried. Every item has a different price, cooks are bustling in the kitchen, at the barbeques, and I'm hard of hearing. A man puts in his order and I am standing there staring at him. I'm trying to wrap my head around this. Is he talking about food? Finally, he says, "The Democrats sure are slow."

"Don't take it out on Pam," I say. "She'll be a great mayor."

The young man helping Pam is studying to be a nurse and is excited to be part of her campaign. "He is the future of America," I tell Pam. Optimistic, proactive, nurturing, open. "When you win, put him on your team."

GAY

P: After the thing in the paper about gay marriage—the Supreme Court upheld same sex marriage as a civil right—Gary Abernathy called me up and said, 'I just want to get your thoughts on the decision.' And I said, 'Gosh, I think it's wonderful.' And the question then was, 'Would you marry a gay couple?' I said, 'Yes, I would.' Well, that's all it took. Because my opponent said, 'Oh he would never marry a gay couple.'

S: Your opponent—the guy who is a drug abuser, womanizer, embezzler...

P: And has gay friends. But it's really BAD in Hillsboro because the Bible says it is a sin for two men to lie down together, Leviticus.

S: Leviticus says slave owners are allowed to keep their slaves forever.

P: Gary Abernathy had asked me, can you recommend a minister that might be good to talk about this, and I gave him the name of a local pastor whose church I occasionally attended. Then I read what he said. And I called him and said, 'I'd like to talk with you about your stance on gay marriage.' And he said, 'Certainly, I'd love to talk to you.' So I said, 'Well, I just don't believe God is hateful. I just don't believe that.' He gave me a piece of paper with Bible verses. I said, 'Do you believe that God created everything on earth?' He said, 'Absolutely.' And I said, 'Then my brother, who is gay, was created by God.' He had no answer. I said, 'Everyone is the United States has the same rights.' My brother Jeff told me, 'Pam you lost the election.' My inner circle, my close friends during the campaign said, 'I think you should apologize.'

S: Apologize? About what?

P: Saying that gay marriage was okay. And I said, 'First of all, I'm not going to apologize. And hurt my brother? I'm not going to do that.' And they said, 'Well, okay.'

Election Night

Pam, Betty, and I leave the victory party at the Elks Golf Course to drive out to the Board of Elections to hear the results. Reporters are typing up results as they come in, a radio announcer is on air, poll workers carry voting machines in black bags to rooms in the back.

Black bags with machines that can be programmed are a bad idea for democracy. Ohio has a reputation of voter suppression, scrubbing, purging, blocking, Diebold tinkering with the machines.[66] The voting machines "malfunctioned"—votes were changed, the count wasn't accurate—during a race for Highland County Commissioner, rumor had it. But no one investigated.

Rory Ryan (left), the town reporter, hand delivers the Highland County Press once a week. He finally left the Republican Party. He couldn't take it anymore. I always enjoy stopping in to get the scoop from Rory when I'm back in town. He's a Don Cherry fan.

Don Cherry, David's father, listened for the music inside the culture, set the music free. I heard him live in 1982, with CODONA—COllin Walcott on sitar and tablas, DOn Cherry on pocket trumpet and African instruments, NAna Vasconcelos, multi-percussionist and magician. They took us on a music journey created in the moment, landscapes, images, harmonies, silences, free and composed. Affirmative, complete, action, communion. It was really something.

Free jazz. Go Rory.

Betty Bishop (center) walked all over Greenfield when she was the City Manager and handed out lightbulbs to curb crime. Keep the lights on. It worked! She was not aligned with Pam on abortion or homosexuality, but accepted the differences and worked hard as the campaign manager, and believed in Pam's leadership ability.

Pam, my childhood playmate. We built towns with sticks and acorns, then got buckets of water and flooded our world, creators and destroyers. Pam has courage. The town has vast problems—mescaline, heroin, opioid epidemic, domestic violence, the decline of a once vibrant core to an uptown with five tattoo parlors. How do you shapeshift the dark energy in a place? We can't pretend anymore. Gentrification is a cover up. It's not the 1950s. Pam is brave.

She lost. 1100 to 750. Pam and Betty are surprised. Momentum was in her favor.

"They flipped the switches," I say. "It was probably the gay issue," Pam says.

On The Deck, Sometime Later

S: You spoke your truth, and you lost. And now the mayor is being indicted for stealing money from the city, blaming you for starting a witch hunt, offending the black community in his Facebook post...

FACEBOOK POST

Drew Hastings: "When are people going to figure out that we are in a Revolution in this Country? Blacks have all but formally declared war on Whites...."

Rory Ryan is all over it in the paper.[67]

Steven Williams, Teresa's son, ran against Pam in the primaries. He called for the mayor's resignation. "How can he represent the African American community in Hillsboro after making that statement?" Steven put the word out to attend the December 14th meeting of the Hillsboro City Council. Pam said it was the most exciting city council meeting she's ever attended.

Jaymara Captain read the social media posts out loud to the City Council and asked, "How does that make you feel?" Brent Burns, a military veteran said, "Sometimes the words we say are the worst weapons of mass destruction."

Steven Williams, remembering the 1954 School Fight when his grandmother Sally Williams was a marching mother and taught in the kitchen schools, looked at the City Council and said, "I don't think you realize that a lot of these people in the audience here went through discrimination, that Hillsboro City School district was one of the last in the country, after *Brown v. Board of Education*, to integrate the schools. So I don't think that the council grasps it, I don't think you grasp it."[68]

On The Deck

S: When the Drew drama dies down, then what? This is a big distraction.

P: City Council "tabled" the discussion.

MUSEUM ROOM
2015, HIGHLAND HOUSE, HILLSBORO

"Hello Susan, greetings from Hillsboro." Tim Koehl's Facebook message appears.

"I am very interested to learn more about Hillsboro's contribution to desegregation and your work to codify it. Since returning to Hillsboro to retire I purchased the Paxton Theatre in Bainbridge and joined the board of the Highland County Historical Society. Having shared that, my objective is to introduce myself to you as a resource for the future. I will also continue to research your work and the role of Hillsboro in the early era of civil rights."

"Great to hear from you." I message back, "I have never been to the Paxton Theatre and now I must go! I'm delighted to hear you are on the board of the historical society. I would love to talk with you sometime about the museum. I have an idea about creating a civil rights room."

"Historical Society is revving up!" Tim messages back, "New blood and enthusiasm. Have been talking civil rights. Theatre is going great. It's like walking up steps with a yo-yo!"

Tim invites me to meet the other board members and I share my version of history—*The Hillsboro Story*—what I discovered over the decade of research, personal experience, connections. The first time I went to the Highland County Historical Museum to research the story, I found one file folder in a cabinet upstairs with one article. This group is ready for action. One of the members had seen my play and knew she'd seen something important. They wondered where to begin.

"You need to get the women at the table," I say. "The African American community needs to be part of this from the get-go. I'll contact my collaborators and set it up."

Eleanor Curtis Cumberland, Carolyn Goins, Virginia Harewood, Teresa Williams, and Joyce Clemons Kittrell take their places at the table. The dusty old portraits tilt. Light fills the room. This big moment is the beginning of black and white histories merging through the voices of these Storytellers, in a county museum that is finally going to make space for a bigger history.

Around the table, each woman makes powerful testimony to the injury of the child who wants to learn and grow, but faces massive abuse and rejection.

Carolyn speaks of feeling shut out, how the children were sent up to the doors and shut out. They were the ones who had to experience that for the protest to go forward.

Virginia speaks of the pain of wondering why her mother made her do this. Does she know how this feels?

Joyce speaks of how her mother pushed her to succeed, the pressure, the insult of being sent back two grades, being treated like dummies.

Teresa speaks of feeling hate directed at her and not understanding what she had done to deserve it.

Eleanor speaks of the indifference of the town toward Black history, then, now, how it's time to shake up the rug.

The Kleenex box is well used.

All of the women speak of the strong and determined mothers who did what they had to do to make things better for their children. Imogene Curtis, Gertrude Clemons, Elsie Steward, Sally Williams, Norma Rollins, Zella Mae Cumberland. They stepped up, with their children.

The Children and the Mothers did it together.

The museum commits—Kati Burwinkle, Pamela Nickel, Deb Koehl, Jim Rooney are moving forward to create an exhibit and a repository for documents that shed light on the desegregation struggle in Hillsboro in the early days of the civil rights movement.

Kati writes a grant to the Ohio Humanities for a planning session, and we all come back to the table to start imagining this room together.

Joyce: "The younger people don't understand. Did this really happen in Hillsboro? When they step into that room, it should be something that will really catch their eye. They'll want to hear more about it. And when they hear it, they're not going to say, 'Well I heard it.' They're going to carry on and remember that we, as human beings, have to change."

Focus on the innocence of the children...
Catch their eye...they'll want to know more...
See the truth...
Giant image of the children...
It was a radical action
Expose the racism

Susan: I hope this exhibit is a form of awakening.
Eleanor: The strike of the match.
Joyce: The thing that really strikes me right now is remembering Miss Imogene and my Mom standing and talking over the fence.
Eleanor: That's how it started. Over the fence.

HEALING THE CHILD WITHIN

Joyce: "When we first moved to Webster, I told my mom, I want to be in the band, play the drums. And Mr. Miller said, 'I don't think you should be playing the drum.' I said, 'Well, I want to play the drum.' 'Well, okay.' When we got to the high school, he put me off to the side. And I said, 'How's come I can't be with the other kids?' And finally he put me in another room by myself, and told me, 'In case some other colored kids want to learn, you can show them how to do it.' I told my mom, 'He's not going to let me in the band.'

Susan: "When you unveil racism in the hall of famers, do they get to be in the Hall of Fame?" George Miller was my beloved music teacher. He taught me flute, how to harmonize. "How do we rectify these things? We are all a part of this."

Joyce: "My daughter wanted to play the clarinet. And he wouldn't let her."

"Were any white people willing to stand up and say, this is wrong?" someone asks.

"No," the women respond in unison.

Thich Nhat Hanh, the Vietnamese Buddhist poet, scholar, and human rights activist, was nominated by Martin Luther King Jr. for the Nobel Peace Prize. He speaks to the wounded child. "The wounded child is in every cell in our body. The suffering of that wounded child is lying inside us right now in the present moment."

Sorrow is an opening.

"When I have a child," my son tells me, "I will make sure that child knows that if I am arguing with someone, it is not the child's fault." My actions caused suffering, and I had to hear that, the anger and the hurt.

Toward the end of *Charlotte's Web*, Templeton the Rat brings Charlotte a newspaper clipping he scrounged from the County Fair garbage, so she can write the last word in the web.

"Here," said Templeton, unrolling the paper.

"What does it say?" asked Charlotte. "You'll have to read it for me."

"It says, 'Humble,'" replied the rat.

"Humble?" said Charlotte. "Humble has two meanings. It means 'not proud' and it means 'near the ground.' That's Wilbur all over. He's not proud and he's near the ground."

Thich Nhat Hanh talks about mindfulness as an ally in healing the wounded child. "Just as the suffering is present in every cell of our body, so are the seeds of awakened understanding and happiness handed down to us from our ancestors. We have a lamp inside us, the lamp of mindfulness, which we can light up anytime. The oil of that lamp is our breathing, our steps and our peaceful smile."[69]

The Light within.

June 10, 1864
I churned and made a cheese.
The men thrashed. Maria washed.
The boys hauled in a rick of clover.
No strangers here today.

EMPTY SPACE
JUNE, 2016, WALNUT STREET, HILLSBORO

Webster Elementary, the memory place where it all started, was torn down in April, 2016, and I return in June to
wrap up the investigation. Elsie will be one hundred years
old in a few days. Where she marched is now a big empty space, gone. I have been pondering how I want to photograph the women, a neutral space to bring out each person.
The empty space, where the school used to be, I decide, and
call everyone up. Will you meet me there and dress up for
a semi-formal portrait? They indulge me again. Pam and I
set up lawn chairs, and the women arrive to sit in front of a
space that had once been a barrier and is now wide open. All
four schools in Hillsboro have been torn down. What about
education?

The light is harsh because it's late morning, and I've been
having a few technical issues with my Nikon that are throwing me off, but I figure, "We're here! Another miracle." I look
at the women all sitting there while I putter around, and I
start to cry. Pam gets Kleenex from the car. Everyone is chat-
ting and I'm taking pictures.

Teresa: "So many kids can't even read."

Joyce: "Nowadays grandparents take care of kids. And I
go out to the school, they say you're not the parent."

Teresa: "Karla went out there." Teresa's daughter Karla,
who had just completed a PhD in education, wanted to col-
lect data from the school board related to her research on
African American women superintendents. "She couldn't get
anywhere with the school. They were trying to block her in
every way. He said she was a liability. The Principal."

Susan: "Are young people getting history?"

Elsie: "They don't care. The parents don't care. All they're thinking about is getting out and making money for themselves."

Teresa: "When we were kids, you had to look out for each other. Look out for your brothers and sisters. We had family time at the supper table. We miss out on that. Everybody was at the table. Now days everybody is in their own room. Nobody knows what's going on in the household."

Carolyn: "Everybody's got a cell phone."

After the photo session, we go to lunch at the West Main Street Café uptown, pull a couple of tables together in the center of the room. Two women at an adjoining table are checking us out. "Gee, we feel underdressed for a Tuesday," one of them says, and we laugh. Judge Davis and his wife are sitting at a table nearby and stop on the way out to say hello, especially to Elsie, who turns one hundred in two days and is the talk of the town. Her big birthday celebration at the Senior Center is a surprise party, so we can't mention it.

"I want to thank you for taking care of my parents," Eleanor says to Elsie. "They didn't have anywhere to live when they came in from Samantha, and you took them in. I've never thanked you."

"Well," Elsie says, "That's just what you did."

"Miss Imogene was a wonderful teacher," Joyce tells Eleanor. "She had a heart for God. That strong will. That power. To have a dream, but have the actions with it. She taught the children that we had to have that love. No matter what people do to you, you still have to try to have that love for a person."

"The last time I saw Gertrude," I tell Joyce again, "I was saying goodbye at the door of her house in Wilmington and she said, 'I'm going to pray that you get this story out.' Your mother's prayer has kept me going."

I dab my eyes with napkins. "Thank you."

These women have all gifted me with their memories, expanded my perspective, deepened my understanding of my culture and myself. This is my beloved community. This is what they have taught me.

Elsie Steward Young

UNITY

Elsie:

"It's remarkable the things you can accomplish when you
work together.

God will take of you, send you things you cannot do on
your own.

You have to have other people around,

promote other people and give them more encouragement.

Encouragement and patience. Be patient."

Carolyn Steward Goins

Virginia Steward Harewood

Joyce Clemons Kittrell,
daughter of Gertrude Clemons Hudson and
Plaintiff in the Hillsboro case

IT WILL TAKE ALL OF US

Joyce:

"It took all of us to make this world what it is.

It's going to take all of us to accept the things in the world, and it will take all of us to make it a better world.

Believe in yourself.

If you don't believe in yourself, and step up and take hold, you're not going to make it."

Teresa Williams, daughter of Sally Williams

TRUTH

Teresa:

"Sometimes the things we have to do to help our children grow, they look at it as punishment. If you don't have values, everything is going to go haywire. Even animals protect their young.

"Mom had eleven children. She taught in one of the kitchen schools and only had an eighth-grade education. She was disciplined and patient.

When we came home from school, we had to get homework done first, then chores, then you could play.

Sally Williams

"She taught us to tell the truth. A lie isn't real.
Keep eyes in the back of your head.
She got her GED later, my sister told me. I didn't know
that.
She died at fifty-six."

WORTH

Eleanor:
"Segregation is very much alive, still very much alive,
but it's quieter now, a little bit more dignified.

People that have love in their hearts, that's what's going to
continue to make change. And the young people. The young
people are not going to go for it.

They don't want segregation. That's what's bringing about
change.

You don't know what other people are going through.
We were taught the Golden Rule.

My mother was a determined woman.
She taught us we had worth."

WEB

Did Mrs. Mallory notice that *Charlotte's Web* was a Caldecott winner and chose the book as the primary text for our third grade class?

"A moment later a tear came to Wilbur's eye. "Oh, Charlotte," he said. "To think that when I first met you I thought you were cruel and bloodthirsty!"

When he recovered from his emotion, he spoke again.

"Why did you do all this for me?" he asked. "I don't deserve it. I've never done anything for you."

"You have been my friend," replied Charlotte.

E.B. White's masterpiece was published at the beginning of the civil rights movement. Were these conscious choices? To write a story and read a story about a smart little spider and a sweet, curious pig who become friends, how we seem to be different, but really have everything in common. I watch a spider weave her web. She turns and spins a perfect pattern.

A great mystery.

Windy Hill Farm

CURIOSITY

"If you were Charlotte, what word would you weave into the web to save the world?"

I ask Clara Alfrieda Goodrich.

"*Curiosity*," she says. A story is an unfinished product. We do not have all the information. There is other information. It is important to keep the story alive.

"You lay the foundation and the changes will come."

Trenton Street, Hillsboro, 2003

with Eleanor and me, Cincinnati, 2016

INTEGRATION

Lewis Goins, Lincoln School 50th Reunion, 2006

"Integration set the stage for things to get better and you can see it. You got this white person beside you and he's making A's and B's—which I wasn't smart enough to figure out when I was young because I wasn't interested—and he's gonna step your game up. I've got two grandkids in college because of the opportunities their parents had. Their mommy and daddy believed in education.

"I was sitting on my porch one day and a man pulled up in a little white car. He came up on the porch to ask me if Richard Williams still lived over there across the street.

'Do you know who I am?'

'No Sir, I don't.'

'I'm Phil Partridge.'

'Yes sir, now I do.' Then we shook hands."

FAIR PLAY

Elizabeth and Philip Partridge

Tom Partridge: "I think about him every day. I think he would say it's a wonder it's held up as long as it has. The political system has been sidetracked by very greedy people. The wars. Huge consequence financially, emotionally and all the trouble they've created. He was very much an anti-war person. There are conspiracy theorists, but this is very well managed and paid for through the media. Huge international corporations own our Congress. He saw that a long time ago. A long time ago."

"What word would your father weave into the web, if he were Charlotte?"

"*Fair Play,*" Tom says.

Deep Down

Tom Partridge: "Once I survived that, I became more independent than I would have been. Being outspoken…in terms of my thinking…not being afraid to be in the minority. I think I worked harder in school than I might have. Yeah, extra ambition. I went to college and started working out. I had a growth spurt. And I'm working out and thinking every night, 'I'm going to go back and beat these guys up.' Later I go to my five-year reunion and I'm so much bigger than these guys and they were kind of pathetic. One guy had all his teeth taken out. Maybe that's why I went into dentistry. He looked like a little old man, and I just felt sorry for him.

"People are just absolutely fearful of the unknown. Just absolutely terrified. And it's in every area. It's in academia. People are afraid of new ideas. They're scared to death. You start bringing some new concept to these bright, educated people and they recoil. There's only so much they can take at one time.

"Fear of ? Fear…

"We don't like something different. Deep down.

"Sometimes somebody will go, 'Oh, you're talking about... your dad set fire to the school.' I say, 'Yeah, it's me.' There was a time when that would have given me a chill and I would have been terrified and thought, oh God, what next. I have no regrets."

pause

"There was a time when I did.

"It all made us closer. No matter where we were, we always kept in touch. We were a closer family because of this."

Tom and Joe, riding up to Lima State Hospital for the Criminally Insane with their Mom for a visit with Philip.

Joe and Tom Partridge, Windy Hill, 2016

Legacy

Tom texts, *Be there at 7 sharp!!!* then rolls in late. His partner, Michelle, an embodiment of grace, manages the majestic dinner scene, with everyone pitching in—appetizers, drinks, jokes. The family is gathering for the holiday weekend. We are eating out on the porch overlooking the pond and barns. The place setting is blue. The flowers on the table from the gardens are arranged in blue vases.

Tom's daughter, Vicky, is parenting her two children, nourishing their curiosity, looking at a frog, helping them negotiate their conflicts, reminding them of their "kindness" points, teaching them to respect life, each other, the people they are with, protecting them from unkind words. Philip would be proud of their dignity.

Joe engages the children, who love his dazzling mind and sweet disposition. He may have been in special ops— his Green Beret sits on the human skull he used in dental school, now on a pedestal at the entrance to his home—but he's playful. We laugh.

It's getting dark and I have to negotiate the back roads into Hillsboro, so I leave the party. Tom walks me to the car. "It's a wrap," I say. We hug goodbye. "I've loved every minute with you," he says.

Me too. I have loved every minute. This is the legacy.

Beloved.

Community.

Part of each other.

Part of a greater design of nature.

Windy Hill

Learning

Home movies, found footage

Just before he dies, Dad says, "I'm learning, Susie!"

"What are you learning, Dad?"

"There's more and more and more to life. It doesn't end here." He smiles.

Ohi-yo Great River

GRACE

From the home movies

Mom and I are in the kitchen doing dishes. "Don't go back to the dead," I plead with her in the dream. We are having such a good time together.

After she dies, I find written in a notebook a quote by Grace Paley.

"If you say what's on your mind in a voice that comes to you from your family and friends and street, you'll probably say something beautiful."

From *Little Things I Remember* by Edith Banyas:

Gathering hickory nuts in the fall and picking them out for fudge and hickory nut cake. The strange old man who came in his wagon to sharpen scissors and knives and camped by the creek. Making catalpa leaf dresses on the chicken house roof. Killing the chickens and feeling sorry for them flopping around with no heads, scalding them, picking all the feathers off, taking the insides out, careful of the oil sack, then cutting them up. "Bless its little heart," I used to say when the tiny heart appeared. Slowly frying the chicken in lard and butter until it was brown and crisp. Saving the wishbone. Did our wishes ever come true? Probably not. I always wished for a pony. The first days of spring when you can shed the long underwear that you folded as neatly as possible but still bulged under your long stockings. Shedding it and feeling the cool grass and soft dirt under your bare feet.

VIRTUE
JULY 2, 2016, SENIOR CITIZEN'S CENTER, HILLSBORO

Elsie Steward Young was born on June 30, 1916, and the family is throwing a big community surprise birthday party for her at the Senior Center on July 2, 2016. The devoted daughters—Carolyn, Charlotte, Virginia—sent out three hundred and fifty invitations and emphasized *surprise*. "She knows," says Carolyn. "But we're just acting like it's all about the family."

"She's quick," I say and we laugh. Elsie is always tuned in.

The family flies in from coast to coast for the big celebration on her actual birthday. The daughters and sons go back and forth to the Dayton airport to pick up the children and grandchildren and great-grandchildren coming to Hillsboro to honor the matriarch of their beautiful big tribe. The daughters are organizing the picnic for the family party, being the hostesses and hosts, making the food, *and* organizing the big surprise party for Elsie. "We haven't stopped," Carolyn says. She looks overwhelmed. Lewis is on the front porch with a beer. I'm sympathetic.

"I had no idea it would take this long to make sandwiches," Virginia says. They make seven hundred pulled pork and chicken sandwiches. "Thank you," I tell them at the party. "You are giving the community a great gift. You are great daughters." But I'm not sure they hear me. They're busy with the potato salad and running back and forth into the kitchen.

The room is joy-filled. Hellos. Introductions. Hugs. Photos.

We hang out at the front door like paparazzi, waiting for Elsie to arrive to catch her look of surprise.

She walks in, and for a few seconds I worry that she's going to pass out. Her three sons keep her steady, the daughters meet and greet and go back to the kitchen, everyone drifts around, having a moment with Elsie in her blue suit, like a queen, receiving red roses, having a word with folks, posing for photos.

We eat and visit, see a slide show of Elsie's life, reach for the Kleenex, hear stories from five of her grandchildren—she has thirty-three grandchildren and more than a hundred great-grandchildren—who testify to her strength and loyalty.

Her children sing a song to her and testify to her faith.

Pastors testify to her spiritual vitality. Her son is supposed to recite a poem—a favorite of Elsie's—but he goes blank, so Elsie takes the microphone and delivers the poem, animated and clever, the voice of a mother keeping her kids in line. We laugh. Then she speaks to us from her heart.

"I'm so thankful to know that I've had so many people I have been involved with. And so many—well there's probably twice this many more—I have been around and loved. And I love each and every one of you and thank each and every one of you for your love for me. And thank you for coming. I appreciate everything that has been done for me from my earliest existence into this present time because I never thought I would be over twenty-three."

People laugh, like she's telling a joke. Her face registers a moment of surprise, that her words seem funny to people. She allows the energy to settle, waits, then opens up again to share her beautiful wisdom.

"My Mother passed when I was three years old and she was around twenty-three, and I thought I wouldn't live any longer than that. But God showed me differently. I'm thankful for all He has done for me, all the events I have come in contact with, all those that are here, and those that are not. And I thank you very much."

We each receive a souvenir to mark the occasion—a bookmark with a photo of Elsie and the words from Proverbs 31:10-3:

Who can find a virtuous woman. For her prize is far above rubies.
She considereth a field and buyeth it, with the fruit of her hands she
*   planted a vineyard.*
She is not afraid of the snow for all her household are clothed with
*   scarlet.*
Strength and honor are her clothing; and she shall rejoice in time to
*   come.*
She openeth her mouth with wisdom; and in her tongue is the law of
*   kindness.*

Thank you, Elsie, for marching for us. All of our lives are better because of your efforts.

Thank you for the treasured memories with you.

Driving out to Pike County to the farm where you were raised, stopping at the cemetery.

"After my grandfather bought this place where I was raised, that's when they bought the graveyard. His father and mother and two of their older children were buried at the church graveyard. My parents are buried up there. My first husband and his people are buried up there in the church graveyard."

"Which Creek were you baptized in?"

"Down by Tennison Graveyard. Close to our church that we have down there. They baptized us in the creek. Now it's been kind of re-routed and messed around with and I don't think there's enough water for baptizing. It was pretty good size. There were several of us baptized that day."

The road goes over and around the hills through the cross-roads, over the tracks near a settlement named Nipgen.

"The train came through down the road. We walked down to the station to get our mail. We'd do some trading. Baking powder. Sugar. DTI. Detroit-Toledo-Ironton. Freight train and passenger train. My dad used to work on the train sorting mail during the Christmas holidays. He was gone three or four weeks with that.

Past the old farm.

"They had horses to plough the fields. We didn't have the John Deeres. There was one horse my grandfather used to drive to Chillicothe when he had to pay bills. When they finally got a car, he wouldn't take the car. He got his horse and wagon.

"My grandfather passed in '31. My grandmother died. And then they sold the farm.

"I got married in '33 when I was seventeen. I eloped."

You eloped?

"We (Elsie and James Lester Stewart) left Chillicothe. He came to my aunt's. 'She's going with me.' Of course, we had to stop and get gas. We went straight on down to Portsmouth. Our pastor lived in Portsmouth. We picked up the Pastor. We went to Kentucky. Are your parents here? No. We went to the next town, and I said I was twenty-one. We dropped the Pastor off in Portsmouth and came on home. The next day my Uncle said, 'It took you a long time to get to Chillicothe.' We showed him the papers. He told my Grandma. They called my Dad. He told my stepmom. 'Ain't nothing wrong with those kids, they just ran off and got married.'

"I'd made up my mind, I wasn't going back to school. The principal at the high school was racist."

Elsie is on-stage after the performance of "The Hillsboro Story" at Southern State Community College. I hand her the mic so she can share her thoughts with the town.

"I can look out over the crowd. I have so many friends that I have been around down through my life. Some of them, I know their face, but I don't remember their names. But they are still a good friend. Because they have been good to me. No matter where I go, they all honor me as being a friend to them. I appreciate that. I go to the stores and I see people that work in the stores and they all come up and hug me and thank me for coming. And I'm thankful that people will reach out to each other. It takes a love in your heart to accept."

Memory
July, 1982

I am in Highland County, Ohio, with my mother, Edith, who has introduced me to her second cousin, Catharine Ingersoll, who shows me the diary of Elizabeth Edwards.

Catharine lends me the family treasure for a few days to transcribe. I insert a sheet of my dad's Banyas Pontiac-Cadillac stationery into the manual typewriter to begin, and decide to open the diary to my birth date to see what Elizabeth had noted on this day in 1864.

July 13
Cool, quite pleasant.
They finished cutting wheat about five,
pulled flax until dinner.
No Strangers here today.
Susan is here.

Alley, Hillsboro

Acknowledgements

Every memory holds a gem of truth, in the voice, in the body, in the body of the words.

Thank you to the people in this book who trusted me with their memories, a great responsibility and privilege.

Eleanor Curtis Cumberland's honest voice came straight from her legacy. Imogene Curtis' leadership style was smart, loving, and outspoken. Thank you, Eleanor, for having my back, and allowing our friendship to grow as the story grew. Elsie Steward Young welcomed me into her her memory places and into her heart. Thank you for your gifts. Carolyn and Lewis Goins welcomed me into their home, always. Thank you, Lewis, for your powerful narrative of war, and Carolyn for sharing joys and sorrows easily.

I am grateful to have met Gertrude Clemons Hudson, to have received her blessings and witnessed her self-empowered leadership style, passed on to her daughter, Joyce Kittrell. Thank you, Joyce, for your passionate desire for real action, and for introducing me to Teresa Williams, who stepped into the story to tell her version of events and to honor her steady, courageous mother, Sally Williams. Thank you, Teresa, for your memory snapshots, documents, and honest humor. Deep gratitude to the late Clara Alfrieda Goodrich for her friendship and support in negotiating the tricky landscape between cultures and pointing me toward the bigger history. Thank you, Doris Cumberland Woods, for welcoming me into your home in the early days of this project, offering a word that became woven into the web of the story—*friendship.*

Thank you, Tom and Joe Partridge and the Partridge family, for keeping Philip and Elizabeth alive through your own humor, sharp perspective, and memories. Your welcoming spirits have been a gift and pleasure. Tom, thank you for affirming my work and trusting me with your powerful and tender history.

Thank you, Pam Limes for hosting me all through the years. Our dialogues continue to illuminate these experience that began in our childhoods. Thank you, Connie Gordon Kean, my childhood friend and long-time ally, who strongly influenced this story, and her husband, Michael Kean, whose scholarship on the Hillsboro desegregation battle was a game changer for me. You both are clearly located in the heart of this story.

Thank you to my classmates and friends, Sally Roush Rogers and Tamara Rogers, who appear in this story as if by magic, as if we were back in the fields, investigating the latest discovery. Your smiles and love of justice shine like diamonds. Thank you, Garry Boone, for handing me a major element of this book as the inadvertent archivist. I am grateful for our connection.

The Honorable Judge Nathaniel Jones personalizes the strategic thinking and high-spirited focus of a civil rights warrior and 'activist judge.' Thank you for your time and insights about the legal system, your personal calling to correct it, and the story's political position in history. I am deeply grateful to Dr. John Bryant for his personal support and his stories and the opportunity to bring art and history and scholarship into play through performances at the National Underground Railroad Freedom Center.

Thank you, Dr. Chris Metro, the keen diagnostician and poet-healer who articulates the medicine for a systemic injury at the core of the story. Your studious insights bring healing to my life and the lives of many others.

Jazz and world music composer David Ornette Cherry infused *The Hillsboro Story* and *No Strangers Here Today* with his Watts, free jazz, Afro style. Thank you for your friendship and art spirit through all the versions and dimensions of this story. Dancer/choreographer Gregg Bielemeier helped me shape both stories into visual theatre and transform the outrage and wonder of this history into striking images. Thank you for styling my work, for stepping into the work as a performer, and laughing together through many years of dancing and inventing. Writer and SO&SO co-founder, Louise Steinman, has been a long-time collaborator and inspiration for bringing sharp attention together with a wild imagination, love of culture, and storytelling panache. She has supported both of these works as a curator, director and reader of early drafts. Thank you, dear soul sister. Gwynne Warner was my voice director in the theatre, infusing the stories with her deeply felt love for the people, their mission, the Ancestral cry for justice. Deep bow. Thank you to the Maya Angelou Writers Guild, and especially Lillian Whitlow, for supporting the work through consistent reflection on the process and business at hand.

Anne Dubuisson, my brilliant editor, saw the structural threads of this delicate weaving and helped me shape the multiple voices, monologues and visual choreography into a book. Thank you, Anne. Cait Johnson brought her theatrical and literary swing to her reading of the work. Thank you for helping me see it as a "shapely thing." Thank you, Holly

Thomas, the poet-copy editor of the final draft, who polished the manuscript with her facile eye-heart-head gift of deep listening and clear direction.

Mary Bisbee-Beek loved the people and politics in the story, from the time she first encountered the story as a theatre script. Thank you, Mary, for trusting the form, guiding me through the steps and aiming the manuscript toward Tod Thilleman at Spuyten Duyvil Press. Tod, thank you for recognizing this dance of history as "cultural re-imagining" and for this opportunity to create a documentary art book.

Thank you, Allen Nause, who brought *The Hillsboro Story* to the stage at Artists Repertory Theatre in Portland for a world premier and tour. Thank you, Rainee Angles, the talented theatre director at Southern State Community College, for your support of both theatre works during performances in Hillsboro.

Christopher Rauschenberg and Janet Stein offered their support as viewers of early work, as a conduit to the Brown Foundation, and as supporters of the educational mission during the theatre run. Thank you for your trust and artful gaze over the years.

Thank you, Carl Davis, for documenting the show and supporting the work during the early years in the making, consistently echoing back your love of the people in the story and the courage and mystery at the heart of it.

As a mother and educator, my mission has been to elevate this story to its rightful place in civil rights history, not as an expert, but from a desire to honor a single memory and follow it to its source, to develop a strong personal relationship to history as an investigator, not a consumer, to experience memory as a powerful force of transformation and connection. Ben Earle saw this educational-artistic mission and supported the development of a high school curriculum by the

Portland Public Schools. Deep thanks, Ben, for your financial and spiritual support.

Thank you Pastor Matt Hennessee for acknowledging the work with a Yolanda B. King "Living the Dream" award and for offering a room at the Vancouver Avenue First Baptist Church (Portland) for post-show dialogues after the theatre run of *The Hillsboro Story*. The community dialogues were generously facilitated by former state representative and political leader, Joanne Hardesty. Thank you both for your bridge-building efforts, activist spirits, and for embracing this work.

Thank you sisters, Martha and Rebecca Banyas, who are always in the memory, reflecting the vibrant landscapes, tyranny, hilarity and sweetness of blood ties set in motion on Danville Pike. Thank you, brother-in-law, Michael Hoeye, for your astute reflections and generous gift that paid for my first months in my own writing studio. Thank you, brother John Robert Banyas, for the guest bed in Ohio, for your presence and curiosity as I went to and fro, and for leading me on beautiful hikes through the Appalachian homeland, where the deepest memories live. Our grandparents, Ira Quincy and Grace Lydia Edwards Rhoten, are ever-present in our memories of Ohio, through our own experiences and the stories and images from our beloved parents, Edith and John Banyas, who gifted us with a take charge energy to negotiate the dramas, trust our instincts, and live toward our dreams.

Thank you to my son, Jack Quincy Davis, who has picked up the energy, mirroring back a passion for creative action. Thank you for your dynamic documentation of both theatre works and for joining the clan dance of poets who speak out through the heart of justice. Many blessings on your journey, a source of inspiration to me and to others. Blessings to my niece and nephews, their partners and children, the cousins and uncles and aunts and kin all the way back in time, and the ones on the way in. May the Light continue to illuminate the path.

Thank you, Mary Spahr, for being the guardian of Elizabeth Edwards' diary and for sharing this legacy through your care and love of the objects and history of our forebears.

Thank you, Beloved Friends, who have laughed and cried with me over the years of creating and living the story. I love you all. Thank you for being you, for your point of view, and for caring.

Thank you to the many others who make appearances in the book, shared their talents and stories, and are part of the story's fiber. Seen or unseen, you are threaded into the tale and the soul of the story.

TEXT AND THEATER CREDITS
THE HILLSBORO STORY

Text
Composed from recorded interviews, primary documents, images, family archives, 2003-2012

Interviewees
Natalie Amato • John W. Banyas • Betty Bishop • Garry Boone • Dr. John Bryant • Wesley Burns, Jr. • Dianna Cole • Arlene Cole • Joe Cole • Betty Jackson Cottman • Eleanor Curtis Cumberland • Judge Richard Davis • Carolyn Goins • Lewis Goins • Clara Alfrieda Goodrich • Mary Hackney • Ross Hamilton • James Hapner • Virginia Harewood • Drew Hastings • Gertrude Clemons Hudson • Judge Nathaniel R. Jones • Connie Gordon Kean • Michael Kean • Joyce Clemons Kittrell • Janet Larkin • H. Scott Latimer • Pamela Limes • Dick Lukens • Judge William McClain • Doug McKay • Diana McKay • Dr. Chris Metro • Judge Constance Baker Motley • Dr. Khalil Gibran Muhammad • Beth Partridge • Elizabeth Partridge • Jennifer Partridge • Melinda Partridge • Dr. Thomas Partridge • Valerie Partridge • Col. William (Joe) Partridge • Anne Partridge Richter • Sally Roush Rogers • Tamara Rogers • Wesley Roush • Dr. Bret Ruby • Rory Ryan • Reverend Fred Shuttlesworth • Munea Standingstone • Mary Brown Turner • Jean Wallis • Sheriff Ronald Ward • Betty Wilkin • Buck Wilkin • Teresa Williams • Jeff Wilson • Doris Cumberland Woods • Elsie Steward Young • Dick Zink

The unpublished memoir of Philip Partridge, *If It Ain't Got That Swing*

Elizabeth Conard Edwards, diary from 1864, *No Strangers*

Here Today

Ancestors and Other Skeletons in the Closet, memoir sketches by Edith Banyas

Equal Justice Under Law by Constance Baker Motley

Additional citations in notes and bibliography

Theatre Production

The Hillsboro Story (now Part II, *The Story*), World Premier, Artists Repertory Theatre, 2011, Portland Oregon

Directed by Susan Banyas

Performed by LaVerne Greene, Jennifer Lanier, Page Jones, KB Mercer, Susan Banyas

Music and Soundtrack by David Ornette Cherry

Choreography by Gregg Bielemeier

Lighting design by Peter West

Artistic Director, Allen Nause

Video documentation by Carl Davis and Quincy Davis

The Hillsboro Story toured to Hillsboro, Ohio/National Underground Railroad Freedom Center, Cincinnati//Brown Foundation, Topeka/rural communities in Oregon, 2011-12

No Strangers Here Today

Text

Composed from the Civil War diary of Elizabeth Conard Edwards, primary documents, images, family archives with additional text cited in footnotes and bibliography

Theatre Production, 2004-2008

Dance monologue, Susan Banyas

Live keyboards and soundtrack by David Ornette Cherry

Choreography by Gregg Bielemeier

Vocal Direction by Gwynne Warner

Lighting Design by Bill Boese
Video Documentation by Quincy Davis

"Slavery and War, Then and Now," essay, Susan Banyas, published in *Friends Bulletin*, September 2005; "The Abolition of War," booklet essay, Susan Banyas, produced in conjunction with performance of *No Strangers Here Today*, Lewis and Clark College convocation of graduate students, Portland, Oregon, 2012.

Initially presented as dance essay for "Time and Memory" conference in Cambridge, England for International Society for the Study of Time.

Commissioned by and performed at *Aloud in LA* series, Central library, downtown Los Angeles

National tours to colleges, drug rehab center, off-off Broadway, theatres, Quaker meeting houses in Hillsboro; Portland; NYC; Philadelphia; Washington, D.C.; Waynesville, Ohio.

Support for both works
Writing and research supported by the Robert Rauschenberg Residency Program, Robert Rauschenberg Foundation, Caldera Residency Program, Sisters, Oregon

Theatre productions supported by Regional Arts and Culture Council, Oregon Arts Commission, Puffin Foundation, Oregon Cultural Trust

Curriculum development and educational support from Ben Earle, Christopher Rauschenberg, Janet Stein, Portland Public Schools

SOURCES
PRIMARY TEXT SOURCES

Interviewees and voiced text listed in Parts II and III and in credits

Philip Partridge's unpublished memoir, *If It Ain't Got That Swing*

Edith Banyas, excerpts from unpublished memoir, *Ancestors and Other Skeletons in the Closet*

Elizabeth Conard Edwards, diary from 1864, *No Strangers Here Today*

Cited Texts

Charlotte's Web, Letters of E.B. White, E.B. White

The Elements of Style, Strunk, William Jr. and E.B. White

I, Fellini, Charlotte Chandle and *I'm a Born Liar, film* directed by Damien Pettigrew

Who Killed Hammarskjold?: The UN, the Cold War and White Supremacy in Africa, Susan Williams

Equal Justice Under Law, Constance Baker Motley

Hillsboro Press Gazette, Hillsboro, Ohio

Dayton Daily News, Dayton, Ohio

Cincinnati Enquirer, Cincinnati, Ohio

Cleveland Call and Post, Cleveland, Ohio

Time Magazine, New York City

Jet Magazine, Chicago

The Progressive, Madison, Wisconsin

The New York Times, New York City

ADDITIONAL SOURCES FOR CONTENT DETAIL AND CONTINUITY

Hillsboro, Ohio, A Case Study in School Desegregation, Michael Kean with Dr. William Glatt, Faculty Research Journal, The Ohio State University, January, 1970.

The Modern Totem: A study of home movies, Susan Banyas, visual anthropology study, San Francisco State University, 1982.

Through Brown-Colored Glasses: Desegregation in Hillsboro, Ohio, Shelly Howard, social studies paper, Bowling Green University, 2002.

"*The Story of Lincoln School,*" *five-part series,* Charlotte Pack, *Highland County Press,* 2003.

No Hate Found in This Town: Desegregation in the Hillsboro, Ohio Schools, Rick Heflin, history paper, University of Northern Kentucky, 2007.

Art and Documents

Home movies, 1950s, John W. Banyas
Family photographs and documents courtesy of interviewees and families
Portraits and landscape photography, Susan Banyas
Paintings, Susan Banyas
The Memory Place, visual map designed by Alisa Looney

Film inspirations (partial list)

Good Night and Good Luck, George Clooney
Free Angela and All Political Prisoners, and *Chilsom '72: Unbought and Unbossed*, Shola Lynch
Nostalgia for the Light, Patricio Guzmann
Eyes on the Prize, Documentary series in twelve parts
To Kill a Mockingbird, Harper Lee, adapted for screen by Horton Foote
Amarcord, Juliet of the Spirits, and *81/2*, Frederico Fellini
The Apu Trilogy, Satiyat Ray

Theatre inspirations (partial list)

Quarry and *Education of the Girlchild*, Meredith Monk
Guantanamo, Victoria Brittain and Gillian Slovo, from spoken evidence
Twilight L.A., Anna Deveare Smith
Swimming to Cambodia, Spaulding Gray

BIBLIOGRAPHY

Abu-Jamal, Mumia. *Live from Death Row.* New York: Avon Books, 1996.

Abu-Jamal, Mumia. *We Want Freedom: a Life in the Black Panther Party.* Cambridge, Mass: South End Press, 2004.

Alexander, Michelle. *The New Jim Crow:Mass Incarceration in the Age of Colorblindness.* New York: The New Press, 2012.

Anderson, Sherwood. *Winesburg, Ohio.* copyright 1919. New York: Viking Press, 1958.

Baldwin, James. *Nobody Knows My Name.* New York: Vintage International, 1961.

Ball, Edward. *Slaves in the Family.* New York: Ballentine Books, 1998.

Ball, Jared and Todd Steven Burroughs, editors. *A Lie of Reinvention: Correcting Manning Marable's Malcolm X.* Baltimore: Black Classic Press, 2012.

Biss, Eula. *Notes from No Man's Land.* Minneapolis: Gray Wolf Press, 2009.

Blight, David. *Race and Reunion, The Civil War in American Memory.* Cambridge, Mass: Belknap Press of Harvard University Press, 2001.

Boggs, Grace Lee. *The Next American Revolution: Sustainable Activism for The Twenty-First Century.* Berkeley and Los Angeles: University of California Press, 2011.

Bordewich, Fergus M. *Bound For Canan: The Underground Railroad And The War For the Soul of America.* New York: Amistad/HarperCollins, 2005.

Braden, Anne. *The Wall Between.* Monthly Review Press, 1958.

Branch, Taylor. *Parting the Waters, America in the King Years, 1954-63.* New York: Simon & Schuster, 1988.

Bresson, Henri Cartier. *The Mind's Eye: Writings on Photography and Photographers.* New York: Aperture, 1999 and 2005.

Chomsky, Noam. *Who Rules the World?* New York: Metropolitan Books, 2016.

Clinton, Catherine. *Harriet Tubman, The Road to Freedom.* New York: Little, Brown and Co., 2004.

Coates, Ta-Nehisi. *The Beautiful Struggle.* New York: Spiegel & Grau, 2008.

Coates, Ta-Nehisi. *Between the World and Me.* New York: Spiegel & Grau, 2015.

Cockburn, Andrew. *Kill Chain: Drones and the Rise of the High-Tech Assassins:* New York: Henry Holt and Company, 2015.

Collier, Jr., John. *Visual Anthropology: Photography As A Research Method.* New York: Holt, Rinehart and Winston, 1967.

Comfort, W.W. *William Penn And Our Liberties.* Philadelphia: Penn Mutual Life Insurance Company, 1947.

Davis, Angela Y. *Are Prisons Obsolete?* Toronto: Seven Stories Press, 2003.

Davis, Angela Y. *Freedom is a Constant Struggle: Ferguson, Palestine, and the Foundations of a Movement.* Chicago: Haymarket, 2016.

Diamond, Elin. *Performance and Cultural Politics.* London: Routledge, 1996.

Dillard, Annie. *An American Childhood.* New York: Harper & Row, Publishers, 1987.

Douglass, Frederick. *On Slavery and The Civil War.* New York: Dover, selections from his writings, 2003, originally published in 1945 by International Publishers Co.

Douglass, Frederick. *Narrative of the Life of An American Slave.* Cambridge, Mass: Harvard University Press edition, 1960, originally published in 1845.

DuBois, W.E.B. *The Souls of Black Folk.* New York: Penguin Signet, 1995, originally published in 1903.

Dunbar-Ortiz, Roxanne. *An Indigenous Peoples' History Of The United States.* Boston: Beacon Press, 2014.

Dyson, Michael. *April 4, 1968*. New York: Basic Civitas Books, 2008.

Fitzgerald, John. *A Peaceable Pilgrimage*. Leesburg, Ohio: Frederick Press, 2002.

Fosl, Cate. *Subversive Southerner*. New York: Palgrave/Macmillan, 2002.

Frank, Robert, introduction by Jack Kerouac. *The Americans*. Germany: Steidel edition, 2008. First edition published in 1958 by Robert Delprire.

Gardner, Alexander. *Gardner's Photographic Sketchbook of the American Civil War*. New York: Delano Greenidge Editions, 2001; first published in two volumes by Philip and Solomons, Washington, D.C., 1866.

Gillon, Steven M. *Separate and Unequal: The Kerner Commission and the Unraveling of American Liberalism*. New York: Basic Books, 2018.

Goldman, Roger and Daniel Gallen. *Thurgood Marshall, Justice for All*. New York: Carroll & Graf Publishers, 1992.

Grant, Ulysses S. *Personal Memoirs of U.S. Grant*. London: Sampson, Low, Marston, Searle, and Rivington, 1885-86. New York: De Capo Press, 2001.

Green, Melissa Faye. *Praying for Sheetrock*. Cambridge: First Da Capo Press, 2006.

Greenberg, Jack. *Crusaders in the Courts*. New York: Basic Books, 1994.

Griffin, Susan. *Wresting with the Angel of Democracy*. Boston: Trumpeter Books, 2008.

Hagedorn, Ann. *Beyond the River*. New York: Simon and Schuster, 2002.

Haley, Alex. *The Autobiography of Malcolm X*. New York: Ballantine Publishing, 1964.

Hall, Stuart and Mark Sealy. *Different: Contemporary Photographers and Black Identity*. London: Phaidon Press Limited, 2001.

Hamilton, Ross. *The Mystery of the Serpent Mound.* Berkeley: North Atlantic Books, 2001.

Hammarskjöld, Dag. *Markings.* New York: Alfred A. Knopf, Inc. (first English edition), 1964.

Harris, Alex and Margaret Sartor, editors. *Gertrude Blom Bearing Witness.* Chapel Hill: The Center for Documentary Photography, Duke University, 1984.

Hedges, Chris. *War is a Force that Gives Us Meaning.* New York: Anchor Books/Random House, 2003.

Hobbs, Robert. *Mark Lombardi: Global Networks.* New York: Independent Curators International, 2003.

hooks, bell. *Art on My Mind: Visual Politics.* New York: New Press/W.W. Norton, 1995.

Hoose, Philip. *Claudette Colvin: Twice Toward Justice.* New York: Farrar Strauss Giroux, 2009.

Irons, Peter. *Jim Crow's Children.* New York: Penguin Books, 2002.

Jensen, Robert. *The Heart of Whiteness.* San Francisco: City Lights, 2005.

Johnson, Paula C. *Inner Lives/Voices of African American Women in Prison.* New York: New York University Press, 2003.

Jones, Edward P. *The Known World.* New York: Amistad/HarperCollins, 2003.

Jones, Nathaniel R. *Answering the Call.* New York: The New Press, 2016.

Kennedy, Adrienne. *People Who Led to My Plays.* New York: Alfred A. Knopf, 1987.

Klein, Naomi. *No Logo.* New York: Picador, 1999.

Kozol, Jonathan. *The Shame of the Nation: The Restoration of Apartheid Schooling in America.* New York: Three Rivers Press/Random House, 2005.

Lapham, Lewis. *Theatre of War.* New York: New Press/W.W. Norton, 2002.

Lange, Dorothea and Taylor, Paul Schuster. *An American Exodus*. New York: Regal and Hitchcock, 1939.

Lin, Shi Khan and Perez, Tony. *Scottsboro Alabama, A Story in Linoleum Cuts*. New York: New York University Press, 2002, originally created in 1935, found in the personal papers of journalist Joseph North.

Lofgren, Mike. *The Deep State: The Fall of the Constitution and the Rise of a Shadow Government*. New York: Viking, 2016.

Manis, Andrew. *A Fire You Can't Put Out, Reverend Fred Shuttlesworth*. Tuscaloosa: The University of Alabama Press, 1999.

Marble, Manning. *Malcolm X: A Life of Reinvention*. New York: Viking. 2011.

Marsh, Charles. *The Beloved Community*. Cambridge: Basic Books, 2005.

McFeely, William. *Frederick Douglass*. New York: W. W. Norton & Co, 1991.

Milton Meltzer. *There Comes a Time, The Struggle for Civil Rights*. New York: Random House, 2001.

Miller, Henry. *Remember to Remember (The Air-Conditioned Nightmare)*. New York: New Directions, 1947.

Mora, Gilles and John T. Hill. *Walker Evans: The Hungry Eye*. New York: Harry N. Abrams, Inc., 1993.

Morrison, Toni. *Beloved*. New York: Alfred Knopf, 1987.

Morrison, Toni. *Playing in the Dark*. Cambridge: Harvard University Press, 1992.

Morrison, Toni. *Remember The Journey to School Integration*. Boston: Houghton Mifflin Company, 2004.

Motley, Constance Baker. *Equal Justice Under Law*. New York: Farrar, Straus and Giroux, 1998.

Muhammad Khalil Gibran. *The Condemnation of Blackness*. Cambridge: Harvard University Press, 2010.

Myerhoff, Barbara. *Number Our Day: A Triumph of Continuity and Culture Among Jewish Old People In An Urban Ghetto*. New York: First Touchstone Edition/Simon and Schuster, 1980.

Naslund, Sena Jeter. *Four Spirits*. New York: William Morrow/HarperCollins, 2003.

Orfield, Gary. *Dismantling Desegregation: The Quiet Reversal of Brown v. Board of Education*. New York: The New Press, 1996.

Orkin, Ruth, *Ruth Orkin: A Retrospective*. International Center of Photography. New York: Mary Engle, The Estate of Ruth Orkin, 1995.

Orwell, George. *Why I Write*. London: Gangrel, 1946. New York: Penguin Books, 2005.

Painter, Nell Irvin. *Sojourner Truth: A Life, A Symbol*. New York: W.W. Norton & Co., 1996.

Parker, John P. *His Promised Land*. New York: W.W. Norten & Co, 1996, oral history recorded in 1880 by journalist Frank M. Gregg, in Duke University archives.

Pepper, William F. *An Act of State: The Execution of Martin Luther King*. London: Verso, 2003.

Rehak, Melanie. *Girl Sleuth: Nancy Drew and the Women Who Created Her*. Orlando: Harcourt Books, 2005.

Rhoades-Pitts, Sharifa. *Harlem is Nowhere: A Journey to the Mecca of Black America*. New York: Little, Brown and Company, 2011.

Russell, Thaddeus. *A Renegade History of the United States*. New York: Free Press, Simon and Shuster, 2010.

Sander, August. *August Sander Photographs of an Epoch*. New York: Aperture monograph in conjunction with Philadelphia Museum of Art exhibition, 1980.

Scahill, Jeremy. *Dirty Wars: The World is a Battlefield*. New York: Nation Books, 2013.

Siebert, Wilbur H. *The Underground Railroad in Ohio* and *Fugitive Slave Laws*. Originally published in 1898 by the Ohio Archaeological and Historical Publications, © in 1993 by A.W. McGraw; Siebert papers at Yale University.

Snider, Wayne. *All In The Same Spaceship*. New York: Vantage Press, 1974.

Steel, Lewis M. *The Butler's Child.* New York: Thomas Dunne Books, 2016.

Strunk, William Jr. and E.B. White. *The Elements of Style.* New York: MacMillian Publishing Company, 1932.

Surgue, Thomas J. *Sweet Land of Liberty: The Forgotten Struggle for Civil Rights in the North.* New York: Random House, 2008.

Terkel, Studs. *Race.* New York: Anchor Books/The New Press, 1992.

Thompson, Heather Ann. *Blood in the Water: The Attica Prison Uprising Of 1971 And Its Legacy.* New York: Vintage Books, 2017.

Truth, Sojourner, edited by Margaret Washington. *Narrative of Sojourner Truth.* New York: Vintage Classic/Random House, 1993, originally published in 1850.

Turse, Nick. *Tomorrow's Battlefield: US Proxy Wars and Secret Ops in Africa.* Chicago: Haymarket Books, 2015.

Waldi, D.J. *Holy Land: A Suburban Memoir.* New York: W.W. Norton & Company, 1996.

Walker, Kara. *Pictures from Another Time.* Ann Arbor: University of Michigan Museum of Art, in conjunction with exhibition Kara Walker: *An Abbreviated Emancipation* (from *The Emancipation Approximation*), 2002.

Weems, Carrie Mae. *The Hampton Project.* Williamstown: Aperture in association with Willams College Museum of Art, 2000.

Weems, Carrie Mae, *Ritual and Revolution* and Rothenburg, Ellen, *Beautiful Youth,* Mary Drach McInnes, introduction. *Telling Histories.* Seattle: University of Washington Press, 1999.

West, Cornell. *Race Matters.* New York: Vintage/Random House, 2001.

Wheat, Ellen Harkins. *Jacob Lawrence: American Painter.* Seattle: University of Washington Press, 1986.

White, E.B. *Charlotte's Web*. New York: Harper Collins, 1952.

Whitehead, Colson. *The Underground Railroad*. New York: Doubleday, 2016.

Whitney, Joel. *Finks: How the CIA Tricked the World's Best Writers*. New York: OR Books/Counterpoint Press, 2016.

Williams, Juan. *Eyes on the Prize*. New York: Penguin, 1987.

Williams, Susan. *Who Killed Hammarskjold? The UN, the Cold War and White Supremacy in Africa*. London: C. Hurst & Co., 2011.

Wise, Tim. *White Like Me*. Berkeley: Soft Skull Press/ Counterpoint, 2008.

Wodiczko, Krzysztof. *The Abolition of War*. London: Black Dog Publishing, 2011.

Wolfe, Thomas. *You Can't Go Home Again*. Cutchogue, NY: Buccaneer Books, 1934.

Woodson, Jacqueline. *brown girl dreaming*. New York: Puffin, 2014.

Wright, Paula Kitty. *Gist's Promised Land: The Little-Known Story Of The Largest Relocation of Freed Slaves In U.S. History*. Seaman, Ohio: Sugar Tree Ridge Publishing, 2013.

Zinn, Howard. *A People's History of the United States*. New York: Perennial/HarperCollins, 1980 and 1999.

ENDNOTES

The Quest

1   Alex Harris and Margaret Sartor, *Gertrude Blom, Bearing Witness*, Duke University, The Center for Documentary Studies.

2   Michael Kean, PhD in Education, with Dr. William Glatt, *Hillsboro, Ohio, A Case Study in School Desegregation, Faculty Research Journal*, The Ohio State University, January, 1970.

The Story

3   Roger Goldman with David Gallen, *Thurgood Marshall: Justice For All* (New York: Carroll & Graff Publishers, Inc., 1992), 147.

4   Louie Robinson, "The Northern City That Bars Negroes from School," *Jet Magazine* March 22, 1956.

5   Juanita Nelson, "A Tale of Fire and Segregation," *The Progressive,* November 1955.

6   Tamara Rogers, writing project/training at Center for Victims of Torture in Minneapolis

7   Roger Goldman, *Thurgood Marshall*, 162.

8   Constance Baker Motley, *Equal Justice Under Law* (New York: Farrar, Strauss and Giroux, 1998).

9   "Holdout in Ohio," *Time Magazine*, April 23, 1956.

The Backstory

10   *Letters from Mississippi*, edited by Elizabeth Sutherland Martinez, with a foreward by Julian Bond (Brookline, MA, Zephyr Press). Student Non-violent Coordinating Committee. SNCC was founded in 1960 to break through fear and forge a new political party—the Mississippi Freedom Democratic Party--with a progressive platform that included health, education, and black empowerment. The leaders—James Foreman, Marion Berry, John Lewis, Stokley Carmichael, Robert Moses, Ella Baker —developed strategies to build a serious "social revolution" in the words of John Lewis. Annie's letter is on page 58.

11   Klansman Edgar Ray Killan was found guilty of manslaughter on June 23, 2005, 41 years after the murder of the civil

rights workers. Ronald Reagan opened his 1980 Presidential campaign in Philadelphia, Mississippi in a speech upholding "states' rights."

12   Annie Popkin was a founding Mother of Bread and Roses, one of the first women's liberation groups. Her photography appears in *Our Bodies Ourselves*, a defining text for the empowerment of women. She is a body-mind therapist and teaches workshops and classes in unlearning racism.

13   Dr. Martin Luther King, Jr., "Beyond Vietnam," Stanford University/The Martin Luther King, Jr. Institute, 1967.

14   William Pepper, *An Act of State: The Execution of Martin Luther King* (London: Verso, 2003). Details of what emerged before and during a civil trial by the King family—that Dr. King was assassinated by agents of the state. James Earl Ray was exonerated by the court posthumously.

15   Fritz Pearls *Gestalt Therapy Verbatim* (New York; Bantum Books,1969) 56.

16   Susan Williams, *Who Killed Hammarskjold? The UN, The Cold War And White Supremacy in Africa* (London:Hurst and Co, 2011).

17   Susan Williams, *Who Killed Hammarskjold?* 31.

18   Susan Williams, *Who Killed Hammarskjold?* 26-27.

19   Susan Williams, *Who Killed Hammarskjold?* 41.

20   Susan Williams, *Who Killed Hammarskjold?* 239.

21   video interview with Dr. Manning Mrable, *Malcolmology*

22   Malcolm X, *The Autobiography of Malcolm X as Told to Alex Haley* (New York, Random House, 1964).

23   Alex Haley, *The Autobiography of Malcolm X*, 500.

24   Editorial, "Malcolm X," *New York Times,* February 22, 1965.

25   "Death and Transfiguration," Time Magazine, March 5, 1965.

26   Malcolm X, Alex Haley, *The Autobiography of Malcolm X*, 495.

27   Paul Coates, *A Lie of Reinvention: Correcting Manning Marable's Malcolm X* (Baltimore: Black Classic Press, 2011), editor's note, 4.

28   Jared Ball interview with Zak Kondo, April 11, 2011, *A Lie of Reinvention,* 228.

29   U.S. Senate Celect Committee to Study Governmental Operations with Respect to Intelligence Activites, Senator Frank Church, chair.

30   Victoria Brittain, "Africa: A Continent Drenched in the Blood of Revolutionary Heroes," *The Guardian,* January 17, 2011.

31   Victoria Brittain, "Africa: A Continent Drenched in the Blood of Revolutionary Heroes," *The Guardian,* January 17, 2011.

32   Joel Whitney, *Finks: How the CIA Tricked the World's Best Writers* (New York: OR Books, 2016), 249.

33   Dag Hammarskjold, *Markings* (New York: Alfred A Knopt,1964), 222.

34   Jo Becker/Scott Shane, "Secret 'Kill List Proves a Test for Obama's Principles and Will," *New York Times,* May 29, 2012.

35   James Bamford, "The NSA Is Building the Country's Biggest Spy Center (Watch What You Say), *Wired,* March 15, 2012.

36   Nick Turse, "Secret Ops Revealed: The US Military in Africa," Tom Dispatch, March 27, 2014

37   Luke, Harding, acceptance speech for Ridenhour Prize for Truth Telling, National Press Club, Washington, DC, excerpted from "Speaking Truth to Power," *The Nation,* May 26, 2014.

38   James M. McPherson, "Top Gun," *The Nation,* June 14, 2004.

39   Constance Baker Motley, *Equal Justice,* 188, 189. Byron De La Beckwith, a Mississippi Klansman and white supremacist, was finally charged with the assassination of Medgar Evers in 1994 and died in prison in 2001.

40   John Lewis, "Representative John Lewis Remembers Judge Constance Baker Motley," Congressional news release, September 30, 2005.

41   Constance Baker Motley, *Equal Justice,* 91.

42   Betty Medsger, *The Burglary,* (New York: Alfred A. Knopf, 2014) and the docu-drama, *1971,* directed by Johanna Hamilton, released in 2014, illuminate these events.

43   Don Van Natta Jr., "Traces of Terror: Surveillance; Gov-

ernment Will Ease Limits on Domestice Sping by F.B.I.", *New York Times,* May 30, 2002.

44   James Bamford, "Post-September 11, NSA 'Enemies' Include Us," *Politico,* September 8, 2011.

45   William Pepper, *An Act of State,* 43.

46   *US Senate Select Committee to Study Governmental Operations with Respect to Intelligence Activities,* chaired by Senator Frank Church, 1976.

47   Mumia Abu Jamal, *We Want Freedom, a Life in the Black Panther Party.* (Cambridge: South End Press, 2004.), 135.

48   *Milliken v. Bradley, 1974.*

49   Edith Green, a liberal Senator from Oregon, led this attack on busing.

50   Jane Littleton, "Unity: Peaceful Acceptance of Desegregation Depends On It, School Consultant Says," Dayton: *The Journal-Herald,* July11, 1975.

51   Paul Turk, "Glatt Sensed Trouble Ahead," *The Journal Herald,* September 20, 1975.

52   Larry Kinner, "Job Nobody Wants," *Dayton Daily News,* September. 19, 1975.

53   Nathaniel R. Jones, *Answering the Call,* (New York: The New Press, 2016), 161-63.

54   *Organic Nation Listening Club,* performance, recorded music, storytelling and live jazz, conceived and directed by David Ornette Cherry in collaboration with multiple jazz artists, poets, dancers.

55   Diane Ravitch, former Secretary of Education under George W. Bush, "Time for Congress to Probe Bill Gates' Education Coup," Diane Ravitch.com, June 9, 2014 and "How Bill Gates Pulled off the Swift Common Core Revolution," *Washington Post,* June 7, 2014. Judge Jones said she acted as an "echo chamber for opponents of desegregation." (*Answering the Call,* 200).

56   Ann Hagedorn, *Beyond the River, the Untold Story of the Heroes of the Underground Railroad* (New York, Simon & Shuster). Her book focuses on the URRR in this area, relative to the great national movement.

57   Fergus M. Bordewich, *Bound for Canaan, The Underground Railroad and the War for the Soul of America* (New York: Amistad/HarperCollins) 373.

58   Nixon appointed four Supreme Court justices during his Presidency including anti-segregationist, William Rehnquist, who was elevated to Chief Justice by Reagan.

59   Judge Nathaniel R. Jones, *Answering the Call*, 96.

60   *Report of the National Advisory Commission on Civil Disorders (Kerner Report)*, 1968.

61   Nathaniel R. Jones, *Answering the Call*, 88.

62   William P. Jones, "Freedom for Every Citizen:The Missed Opportunity of the Kerner Report," *The Nation*, April 30, 2018.

63   Quincydavismusic.com. Quincy Davis' video documentary, *Subconconsious War* (2011) is a riveting 30 minutes of "found footage" that inter-cuts live video recording of a U.S. helicopter attack on innocent Iraqi civilians, leaked to the press by Chelsea Manning, with ultra-violent first person shooter video games, targeted for children, with backdrops in the Middle East. Commentary by Marshall McLuhan, Neil Postman, Aldous Huxley, John Trudell, and the American soldier who rescued two Iraqi children shot and wounded during the attack.

Beloved Kaleidescope Community

64   Grace Lee Boggs, *The Next American Revolution: Sustainable Activism for the Twenty First Centry* (Berkeley: University of California Press).

65   Grace Lee Boggs, interview with Amy Goodman and Juan Gonzales, *Democracy Now,* April 14, 2011.

66   Mark Crispin Miller's "None Dare Call It Stolen: Ohio, The Election and America's Servile Press," *Harpers*, August 2005. Greg Palast, "How They Stole Ohio," blog, June 2, 2006.

67   Rory Ryan,"Council Must Censure This Mayor," *Highland County Press*, December 3, 2015.

68   Caitlin Forsha, Mayor, "City Council Lambasted as Citizens Call for Action," *Highland Co Press*, December 15, 2015.

69   Thich Nhat Hanh, "Healing the Child Within," *Shambhala Sun*, March 2011.

ASTORIA, OREGON, PHOTO BY QUINCY DAVIS

SUSAN GRACE BANYAS is a multi-media artist and choreographer.
She was raised in Southern Ohio and lives on the West Coast.
This is her first book.

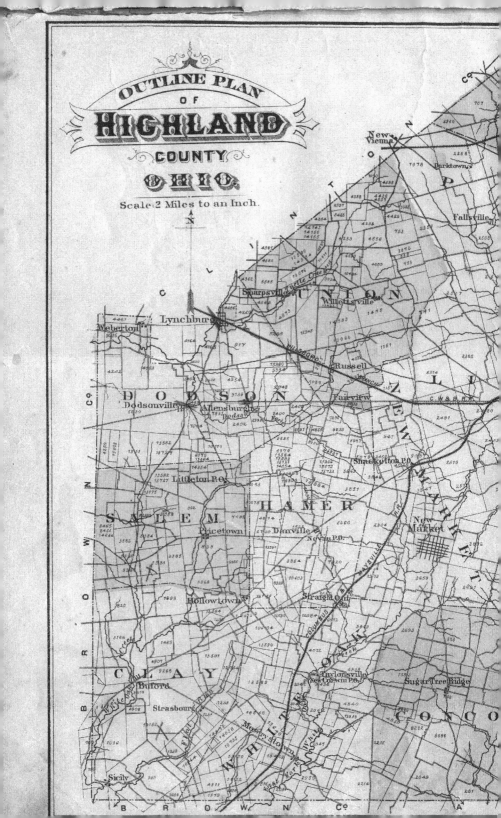

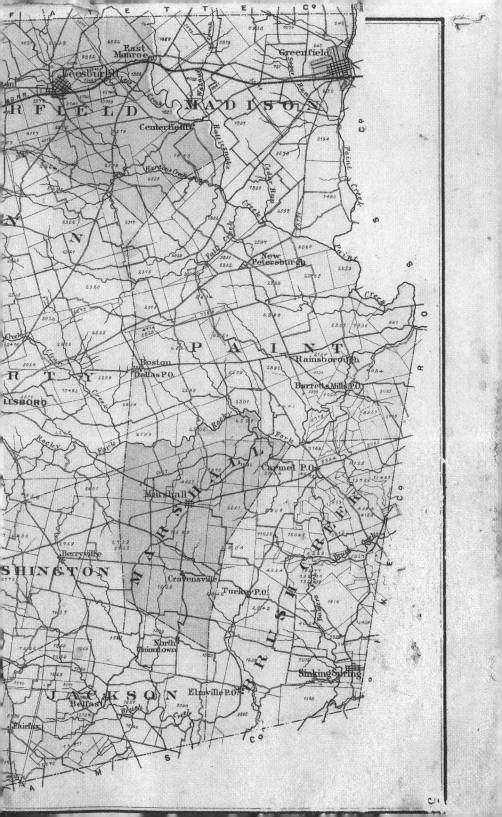

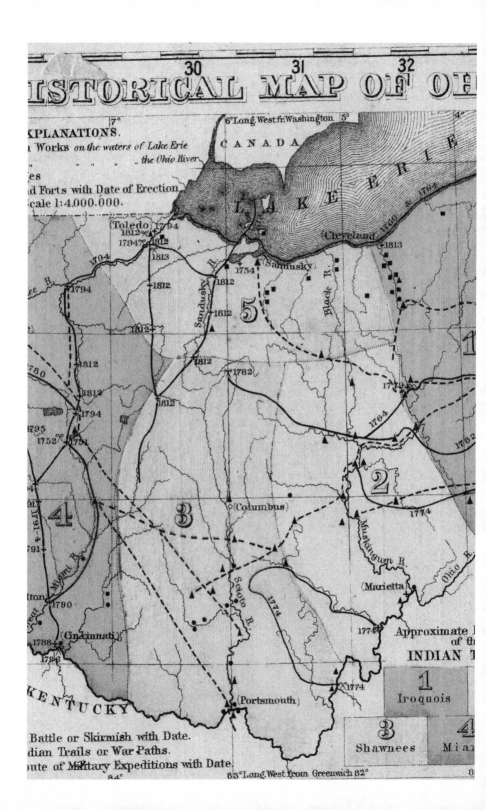

HISTORICAL MAP OF OHIO

EXPLANATIONS.
n Works *on the waters of Lake Erie*
                    " *the Ohio River*
es
d Forts with Date of Erection
Scale 1:4.000.000.

6° Long. West fr. Washington   5°

C A N A D A

L A K E   E R I E

1769 & 1764

(Toledo) 1794
1812
1794 × 1812
1813
(Cleveland) 1769 & 1764
+1813

1794
1813
(Sandusky)
1754
+1812
ee R.
1794
+1812
Sandusky R.
+1812
5
Black R.

+1812
1780
+1812
+1812
+1782
1779

1812
1812
1794
1764
1762

1795
1752 ×
1751

1
(Columbus)
2
1774
1791-4
4
3
Muskingum R.
1774
1791+
Miami R.
(Marietta)
Ohio R.
Scioto R.
Approximate
of th
INDIAN T

lton 1790
1774
1774
1788
(Cincinnati)
1786
1   Iroquois

K E N T U C K Y
(Portsmouth)

Battle or Skirmish with Date.
dian Trails or War Paths.
oute of Military Expeditions with Date.
84°   83° Long. West from Greenwich 82°   8

3   Shawnees   4 Miar

Made in the USA
San Bernardino, CA
25 January 2020